DO YOU TAKE GOD?

Committing to God's design for marriage

Eric L. Owens

ISBN: 1519763727
ISBN 13: 9781519763723

This book is dedicated to my wife, Vanessa. Honey, thank you for saying yes more than twenty-seven years ago. Thank you for three beautiful daughters who you have helped turn into three beautiful women. I will never forget that you sang at our wedding, the song was, "You bring me joy" by Anita Baker. You sang it to me and it was beautiful, I hope that I have been true to those words, because you have given me joy.

In the seventh grade we became friends, I appreciate our friendship - you will always be my bestie. I thank God for our marriage and all that it has meant to both of us. What an adventure it has been, we have grown up together and by the grace of God we are still growing together. I look forward to growing old together. We will be those little old people holding onto each other and helping each other.

When we are old and looking back on our life, my greatest joy will have been to walk through life with you.

I love you.

Eric

TABLE OF CONTENTS

INTRODUCTION

I married my best friend in 1988, in a small church where I was reared and she obeyed the gospel. That was a long time ago and since then, I have learned a lot about myself, my wife, and marriage. We have had a good marriage. However, it has not been without its ups and downs. Through the years, we have both hurt and helped each other. We reared three beautiful daughters and moved numerous times. We have overcome challenges, suffered setbacks, and endured our share of heartbreaks. We have been married and it has grown sweeter, and better the closer we've gotten to God.

When God created the world, the only thing he announced as not good, was man being alone. Our heavenly Father solved the issue by creating a woman and thus generously giving humanity marriage. The union of marriage is of divine origin. Marriage is created and governed by God, but man has been constant in his refusal to follow God's divine instructions.

God determined that a man and a woman were to be married and each was to function in a role within marriage. According to God, the husband is the head of his wife and the wife is to submit to her husband. Man in his wisdom has proclaimed God's design as outdated, old and sexist, is it?

Our rejection of God's design has resulted in difficulties and divorce. Today it is more likely for women to lead families then men. Or for men and women to fight over who will lead and direct the family. Husbands and wives are often unhappy and unfulfilled in their marriages. With many opting to divorce rather than to keep struggling.

What if we return to God's design? Can God help our marriages, of course he can? If we reject cultures notion of no one leading the home or women leading the home, our marriages will be blessed. If men led like God, lived like Christ and loved their wives like Christ loved the church, our marriages would be blessed. God never intended for marriage to be endured, tolerated, or survived. He had so much more planned for us.

The purpose of this book, is to exhort us to return to God's design for marriage. Reject our cultures disagreement with God and allow God to bless our marriages. The book is divided into four sections: Section one is for the couple: for us. This section details God's design and intention when he created marriage. It will be in stark contrast with our cultural teaching on men and women and their roles in marriage. Section two is for him. Christ is the man's example for how to be a husband. If a man will be the husband God wants him to be, he must act toward his wife like Christ behaves toward the church.

Section three is for her: The church is the woman's example for how to be a wife, she is the bride of Christ. God's instruction to a wife is very different than what women hear and learn growing up in our culture. If a woman will be thew wife God desires she will focus more on her inner beauty than her outer beauty.

Section four is for us. This section contains practical helps and tips for the couple. We can have the marriages we desire and God intended by taking God's word and emulating him. Of course he can read her sections and she can read his. It might actually help to get the other person's perspective. Plus, after you read your section I'm sure you will want to know what I said to your spouse.

I want to live the happy blessed life God intended for us when he gave us marriage and I trust you want the same thing. So let's take a look backward so we can move forward. Together we can discover or maybe re-discover God's intention when he gave us the great and wonderful relationship called marriage.

SECTION 1

Chapters 1-6

God's Design For Marriage

For Us

1

WE CAN'T ACTUALLY REDEFINE MARRIAGE

Marriage is so important because marriage is from God, marriage is how God revealed himself and his relationship with his people. God was married to ancient Israel and Christ is married to his church. Because of marriage we understand what God means when he says he is a jealous God. The concepts of faithfulness, oneness and unity we find in marriage begin with God and his people. It is difficult to imagine anyone, who claims to believe in God, suggesting that God would approve of his people having a different husband or redefining the relationship with him.

Marriage reveals more about us and our relationship with God than it ever will about our relationship with our spouse. "Do you take God?" this is the question. We cannot take God's marriage while refusing to take God and we will never be able to have God on our terms.

It is this that makes the US Supreme Court's acceptance of the Lesbian, Gay, Bisexual, Transgender (LGBT) community's argument to redefine marriage so sad and unfortunate. It is beyond the Court's scope and authority to redefine marriage. Man did not define marriage; therefore, he has neither power nor right to redefine it. Legal is not synonymous with *moral, right, or good.* We can either have God or we can have fornication, but we cannot have both.

Fighting against God

Disagreement with the redefinition of marriage is not about highlighting one sin above another, for everyone will or has fallen short of the glory of God (Rom. 3:23). Neither is the disagreement about insensitivity toward the understanding that people struggle. Everyone struggles with something—some more intensely than others, but we all struggle.

Then what is the disagreement with redefining marriage about? Simply put, it is about fighting against God. It is about identity. It is about truth—its existence, recognition, and ability to be understood and proclaimed. You know you're getting old when you begin sentences with the phrase, "I never thought I would live to see the day." Well, I am old because I never thought I would live to see the day when people would argue over what constituted marriage.

We have argued over what makes a good marriage. We've argued over the roles of each person within a marriage. We've argued about what you should do to stay married. We have even argued about whether or not people should get married. But at no point in our history have we argued about what constitutes a marriage. Like the Geico commercials say, "Everybody knows that." Or at least it seems everybody used to know that.

One man and one woman; if this is not your definition of marriage, you have the wrong definition. The originator of marriage has never changed his definition. I'm troubled when I know someone is trying to deceive me, especially when the thing in question is so obvious that not only is my sight brought into question but my intelligence and very existence as well. Life and truth both demand consistency. Redefining marriage is not truthful neither can one be consistent with the arguments that were used.

Then How Can We Know Anything?

To declare that a union between a male and a female no longer exclusively constitutes marriage is utterly ridiculous. Listen, this is not about people practicing homosexuality or lesbianism, both of which are fornication. Though fornication is wrong before God, no one is trying to make anyone not sin. This is about someone looking another person right in the eye and saying that a male and a male can get married to each other or that a female and a female can get married to each other.

Here is what that is like. Imagine you and me walking outside together, taking off our shoes, and standing on the front lawn. We feel the grass under our feet. We walk around in the grass. For a while, we both call it grass, and we acknowledge that it is green. Now for thousands of years, everyone has called this stuff grass. Not simply in our country did they call it grass but everyone, everywhere, in every era has always and only called it grass. According to Genesis 1:11, God created grass on the third day.

Now, how would you feel if one day I came to your house and asked you to come outside to your front lawn? We then took off our shoes like we had before. However, on this day, quite to your surprise, I no longer wanted to exclusively call this green stuff we were standing on "grass". In fact, I now wanted to call the trees "grass" also. And when you disagreed, I argued with you and insisted that the tree was also called "grass". After arguing awhile, I started to refer to you as narrow-minded and bigoted. Soon, others took up my argument, and you began to hear it on the news and read about it in magazines. Grass is no longer exclusively grass, trees are also grass. You even heard that laws were being passed, agreeing with me.

This is what it is like for people to one day decide that the only thing we have ever known as marriage is actually no longer the only thing that is marriage. God created marriage on the sixth day. But now the thing that God created is the exact opposite. This is tantamount to saying up is down, and down is up. The sky is green, and the grass is blue. Scripture warns us about doing this to truth.

Woe to those who call evil good and good evil, who put darkness for light and light for darkness, who put bitter for sweet and sweet for bitter! Woe to those who are wise in their own eyes, and shrewd in their own sight! (Isa. 5:20–21) (KJV).

We all struggle with sin. But if you are going to tell me that two men can marry each other, I just think you should also tell me that trees are fish, and fish are trees. It will make as much sense as the other. If you want to do it, it's still wrong, but it's your choice. But don't try to convince the rest of us that it is now right. I ask you, can we know anything anymore? If a person can change marriage, is there anything that can't be changed? I'll answer; no!

It's Only a Matter of Time

If the pedophile picks up *the exact same line of argumentation* that the LGBT community has argued, what would be the objection to his cause? If one says the age of consent, that's fine, but what if age of consent laws were lowered, as some are seeking to do? What if the Supreme Court decided that the age of consent should be moved to eight, ten or twelve—or be removed altogether? If a lawyer for the position could get before the court, he could argue that children are smarter now, children develop faster now, or children mature much sooner than they once did.

This lawyer could further argue that age-of-consent laws are based on outdated models. Still further, he might suggest that the tradition of what was once unacceptable has become more acceptable. He might even argue that pedophile's are be shamed unjustly. And on and on it would go until those who have argued for the redefinition of marriage for the LGBT community would have to concede to others who use their same line of argumentation.

If you argue that a person can be born a homosexual, how can you argue that another person could not be born a pedophile? Let me ask that another way. If one man could be born attracted to men, why couldn't another one be born attracted to boys? The LGBT community argues that just because a person was proclaimed something at birth doesn't mean that individual has to identify that way as an adult. What if the pedophile used the same argument, will we allow it?

And what about love, you heard the same thing I did, didn't you? Love chooses us; we don't choose love. And love wins! Oh yeah, and what about civil rights? Doesn't the pedophile have rights? How long before the pedophile argues that being a pedophile is just like being black? Before you get too offended consider that homosexuality is fornication and so is pedophilia. If one form of fornication is like being black, why aren't others? Many of these arguments are already being used to remove age-of-consent laws.

The North American Man/Boy Love Association is already actively engaged in this effort. They believe they have a civil right to sexually love children. Their stated mission is to remove the age-of-consent laws. If you supported the LGBT community's redefinition of marriage, how would you say no to NAMBLA? Just take the same arguments—born this way, civil rights, love, suppression, religious hypocrisy, failure of heterosexual marriage, phobias on the part of opponents, like being black or hurting their dignity. If you are honest, if those arguments were applied to NAMBLA, consistency will demand that you join their cause and support their movement—remove age-of-consent laws, decriminalize sex with minors, and release from prison every person arrested and jailed for pedophilia.

If they could get their movement before the Supreme Court, how could the court disagree? At least five judges have shown their willingness to accept these arguments for redefining marriage. Now that the LGBT community has successfully redefined marriage to benefit themselves, wouldn't the Court have to support NAMBLA's attempt to do the same? Or would it allow just one redefinition of marriage; or just one at a time?

Changing the only definition of marriage humanity has ever known removes all certainty and boundaries. Once those are removed, anyone can use the same arguments and change marriage again and again without limit. Not liking it is not enough to prevent it. The majority of people were not for redefining marriage, but that didn't stop it from happening.

A Committed Relationship, Says Who?

I've heard people say that scripture does not condemn homosexuality. They then suggest that God is for committed sexual relationships

7

between people of the same gender. Really? God never endorses fornication, and homosexuality is fornication (1 Cor. 5:1–3; 1 Cor. 6:9–10; 1 Cor. 7:1–5; Eph. 5:3; Heb. 13:4). He denounces it in the strongest language.

Additionally, please tell me why the relationships have to be committed? Why can't they be uncommitted? If we can no longer say that marriage is exclusively between a man and a woman, how can anyone say you must be committed to whomever you marry? Where did we get the idea of commitment in marriage? Maybe the idea of commitment came from God creating only one woman for Adam.

Or maybe commitment came from God's statement that man is to leave his father and mother and cleave to his wife. Though not obvious from Genesis 2 and maybe because Adam didn't have a physical mother and father it seems uncertain who made the statement to leave and cleave. However, in Matthew 19:4-5, Jesus tells us that God told Adam to leave and cleave. The one who made them at the beginning said it.

Commitment is God commanded not man invented or society-imagined. But if that is true, and it is, if one is going to use the Bible and God's creation to say committed relationships are what God intended, then why is one going to ignore the fact that God created a woman for the man and not another man?

No one who seeks to redefine marriage has any basis in trying to regulate it after the redefinition. Since we rejected God's definition and created our own; we can reject one another's new definition and continue to redefine marriage. Why should five judges word be stronger than the word of God? Committed relationships, says who?

We Both Love Her

And where did we get the idea that a marriage should be between just one man and one woman? Of course, I would argue we got that from the Bible and the God who created marriage. Still, those who seek to change marriage also like the idea that it should be with one other person at a time. But on what basis could they hold firm to that position? Suppose two men "loved" the same woman, and she "loved" them both back. They all wanted to get married. Could they—or rather, will we allow them to—marry? This argument is also already being used, just give it time to be successful. Some are also arguing for multiple men and women to be able to get married to each other. If they used the same arguments that succeeded with the court, the court would have no reasonable basis for saying no.

If not, why not? Information about number of partners and the gender of each comes from the same source (Gen. 2:18–25). God made a woman for Adam; he did not make a man. Since they believe it is alright to change one part of marriage why not every part of marriage? It is obvious God did not make two women for Adam, nor did he give two men to Eve. Polygamy was never God's intention, it was man's abuse. The one who made them at the beginning made a male and a female.

If we can no longer clearly identify what constitutes a marriage then what can we identify? Friend, think back in your life and even beyond your life; consider your parents' lives. Did you ever think there would be a day when we would argue that a man and woman is not the only thing that constitutes a marriage? And no less than the Supreme Court would weigh in and attempt to redefine marriage. Could you have imagined it?

The fact that some are willing to ignore the obvious does not change it. Truly, we are casting God off and exchanging his wisdom for ours, we are fighting against God. We think we are wise in so doing, but actually we have become fools. The sad reality is that every society that has acted in this manner in the past has grown worse and worse and ended tragically. The following verses so well describe our time, society and culture that it reads as if it were written today.

> For the wrath of God is revealed from heaven against all ungodliness and unrighteousness of men, who by their unrighteousness suppress the truth. For what can be known about God is plain to them, because God has shown it to them. For his invisible attributes, namely, his eternal power and divine nature, have been clearly perceived, ever since the creation of the world in the things that have been made. So they are without excuse.

For although they knew God, they did not honor him as God or give thanks to him, but they became futile in their thinking, and their foolish hearts were darkened. Claiming to be wise, they became fools, and exchanged the glory of the immortal God for images resembling mortal man and birds and animals and creeping things. Therefore God gave them up in the lusts of their hearts to impurity, to the dishonoring of their bodies among themselves, because they exchanged the truth about God for a lie and worshiped and served the creature rather than the Creator, who is blessed forever! Amen. For this reason God gave them up to dishonorable passions. For their women exchanged natural relations for those that are contrary to nature; and the men likewise gave up natural relations with women and were consumed with passion for one another, men committing shameless acts with men and receiving in themselves the due penalty for their error.

And since they did not see fit to acknowledge God, God gave them up to a debased mind to do what ought not to be done. They were filled with all manner of unrighteousness, evil, covetousness, malice. They are full of envy, murder, strife, deceit, maliciousness. They are gossips, slanderers, haters of God, insolent, haughty, boastful, inventors of evil, disobedient to parents, foolish, faithless, heartless, ruthless. Though they know God's righteous decree that those who practice such things deserve to die, they not only do them but give approval to those who practice them.

Rom. 1:18-32 (ESV)

Instead of learning from the past we seem bent on repeating history. In our own self-will we have sought to redefine God's divine institution of marriage. Since the creation of the world, we have used God's model to identify marriage. And it has blessed our lives and perpetuated our existence, in every culture and era.

When we take that which God condemns and call it something that God allows and endorses, we do this to our detriment as individuals, communities and nations. Marriage is a union between a man and a woman, a male and a female. This is God's definition of marriage and—despite political correctness, the agenda of a few, and the sympathy of others—God has not changed his definition. Please don't lose your soul fighting against God. Love people, struggle with people, pray for people, help people, but don't attempt to change God's Word and his ways for people.

Every time you go outside to your lawn, remember that the green stuff under your feet is still exclusively grass. Should you choose to call a tree "grass," "sue," or attempt to silence those who reject your redefinition, you should know this.

Calling a thing something it is not can never change that thing into something else. Even if the Supreme Court calls a tree grass it's not, it is still a tree. Grass is grass and a tree is a tree. And marriage is only between a man and a woman, a male and a female. Try as we might, we cannot actually redefine marriage.

2

WHAT IS MARRIAGE?
CAN YOU DESCRIBE IT?

There is probably nothing that the world has more wrong than the picture of marriage it paints for little boys and girls. When little girls are dreaming of their wedding days, dresses, and decorations, they have no idea of what comes next. When little boys are watching those beautiful wives in the movies, respond to their husbands' every desire and fantasy. They have no idea how appropriate the word fantasy is. Never has the phrase bait and switch been more appropriate than when applied to ideas we grow up with of marriage.

Little boys and girls grow up with hopes and dreams about marriage. Based on these dreams, they find someone, set the date, and have the ceremony. After a short reprieve from life on a honeymoon, they come back to reality and begin to live in their marriage. And for many couples, the shock of the reality of marriage is great. Sometimes the shock is so severe that some, have buyer's remorse.

In the worst case scenario the shock can look like this:
Imagine a private beach with just you and your love. You sat together on the balcony and watched a gorgeous sunrise. You shared breakfast and stared into each other's eyes. After a relaxing time together, you said, "Let's go walk on the beach."

So, you got your flip-flops and towels and headed toward the beach. Ahead was a clearing, and you had to pass through some beautiful green foliage. You held hands and brushed the branches aside, and as you ducked your heads, your feet touched the sand. No sooner than your feet touched the sand, suddenly and without warning, bombs began to explode.

You both immediately hit the ground. You feel the hot sand, but you can't focus on the heat because of the bombs exploding above your heads. You try, but it isn't safe to lift yourselves up. Now, crawling on your stomachs, you are horrified as you see dead, failed marriages all around you. More shots are fired, and you know they are getting closer to you. You scream for your spouse, but you receive no answer. You feel for their hand, but you can't touch them their hand anymore. Your love is gone, you are separated and fighting for your life alone. You are at war. You are dazed and confused. Flashes of the deck and breakfast race through your mind, but that seems like a lifetime ago.

One word fills your mind, survive. "How can I get through this?" you ask. Survival is the solution: you must find your spouse, seek shelter, get out, fight, or surrender.

The smoke clears, the bombs stop, you stand up and life screams, welcome to marriage!

For many people, marriage is like planning for a trip to the beach but ending up in a war. Often we are simply unprepared to meet the challenges we will encounter. If only someone had told us what we were really getting into. If only we would have listened and not allowed ourselves to make a lifelong decision on a few good feelings. Someone told me a long time ago that there are two things we don't learn enough about. One is money, and the other is marriage. Then he added, "And you can mess them both up real fast." Amen.

This book is about marriage; it's about what we are really getting into when we say "I do." It is about what God intended when he gave us marriage. What did God design it to be? If we get back to what God intended and live in it the way God designed, the beach will be ours and the war a distant memory. So let's start from the beginning, what is marriage, can you describe it?

Suppose that you were visited by an alien. Your task was to teach him about life on earth. To do so you had to describe things on earth for him, because he didn't know anything about our world. You take him outside, and he sees a bird and then a plane, and he asks what they are. You begin to describe them and maybe you start like this: "A bird is a winged animal with feathers, a beak, and two feet. Most of them can fly, but some cannot." You consider your description, proud of the job you did and the clarity you provided your visitor. But suppose he asks you, "What are wings, and what is a beak?"

You begin to describe the plane, and you say that it is a large tube-like machine with wings and huge engines to help it get airborne. It has seats inside, restrooms, and a cockpit for the pilots filled with instruments to help them navigate the plane. It also has a crew and landing gear to land safely. Great description, but can you see how many follow-up questions he might have?

Next, our guest observes a wedding, and he asks what the people are doing. You reply that they are getting married, and he says, "Married? What's that"

Before you answer, please pause here and consider your description—and if you are married, ask your spouse to describe marriage too. If you have children, ask them to describe marriage and then compare your descriptions. Do we know what we have done? Is our description the same? Listen to the picture your children have of marriage? Is your families description God's description?

Since we know what things are, we rarely hear ourselves describe them, and it is precisely this lack of thought and description that can cause many challenges in marriage. When we don't describe and understand what marriage is, we are more apt to use it improperly and expect things from it that God never intended. For most married people, a major problem in their marriage is unfulfilled expectations.

But what if what they expected from marriage was never intended by God when he gave us marriage?

God gave us marriage. We should expect to receive from it only those things that he intended. So we need to ask and answer what did God intend when he gave us marriage. Hopefully, your expectations of marriage are the same as God's intention. The following are some of the things the Bible says marriage is and what it is meant to accomplish. This would not only help our alien visitor, it will also help us.

The Composition of Marriage

Man is a unique creation because only man shares the image of God. Genesis 1:26–27 tells us,

> And God said, Let us make man in our image, after our likeness: and let them have dominion over the fish of the sea, and over the fowl of the air, and over the cattle, and over all the earth, and over every creeping thing that creepeth upon the earth. So God created man in his own image, in the image of God created he him; male and female created he them (KJV).

Notice the last phrase, "in the image of God created he him; *male and female created he them.*" God made a male and a female in his image. Genesis chapter 2 gives us more details about man's creation. We are told in chapter 2:7 that God made man from the dust of the ground and breathed into him the breath of life, and man became a living soul. We are also told that after God made Adam, he said that it was not good that the man should be alone. The person God made for Adam was a woman. Scripture is clear that from the beginning, God created marriage and that the composition of that union is one man and one woman or a male and a female.

When the Pharisees tempted Jesus with a question about divorce, Jesus answered with a reference back to the beginning. Read Matthew 19:3–5:

> The Pharisees also came unto him, tempting him, and saying unto him, Is it lawful for a man to put away his wife for every cause? And he answered and said unto them, Have ye not read, that he which made them at the beginning made them male and female, And said, For this cause shall a man leave father and mother, and shall cleave to his wife: and they twain shall be one flesh (KJV)?

The Lord's answer tells us several things: (1) They should have read it. (2) God made them at the beginning. (3) Marriage is made by and governed by God; it was not created by man neither can it be changed by man. (4) He made them male and female.

When it comes to explaining what marriage is then, you must explain to your alien visitor that the composition of God's institution of marriage is one male and one female. By definition, any other construction cannot be marriage.

Companionship—The Intent of Marriage

If there were one concept that stands out as to why God created marriage, it can be found when God looked at Adam and said, "It is not good that the man should be alone...I will make him a helper fit for him" (Gen. 2:18). The term and concept that should dominate the thoughts of present and future husbands and wives is companionship.

When you are considering marriage, please know that you are choosing someone to share your life with. Expunge from your mind the person's good looks and other niceties and think long term. Ask yourself, "What was not good in the garden of Eden before Eve was created?" Because at the end of days 1-5 of creation, God looked at what he had made and said it was good.

Some mistakenly suggest that Adam was incomplete. Nothing could be further from the truth. The garden was good; the trees were good, the animals were good and Adam was also good. He had no lack in himself; he is not insufficient. Listen carefully to what God said: "It is not good that the man should be *alone*." The thing that is not good in the garden is aloneness. Maybe we shouldn't even consider Adam as being lonely because he had never had anyone to miss. Literally, he is the first man on earth; there were no other humans.

The intent of marriage is so that we don't go through life alone. God provided us marriage so we could share our lives with someone. Marriage provides us strength to keep going and support when we are down. It helps us to enjoy the good times and endure the bad times.

One of the sadder pictures in the world is a human being growing old alone. Many young people want desperately to get away from their spouses. How terribly wrong this kind of thinking is. We won't always be young, God said it was not good that the man should be alone. It still isn't.

Propagation—A Major Purpose of Marriage
God spoke the world into existence:

> By the word of the LORD were the heavens made; and all the host of them by the breath of his mouth. He gathereth the waters of the sea together as an heap: he layeth up the depth in storehouses. Let all the earth fear the LORD: let all the inhabitants of the world stand in awe of him. For he spake, and it was done; he commanded, and it stood fast (KJV).

> —Psalm 33:6–9

The first generation of everything was made by miracle; the second and subsequent generations would be produced naturally. Everything was made to reproduce after its own kind. The seed principle is rooted in creation. The fruit, the animals, and humans all have seeds within themselves. Adam and Eve were married on the day they were created, and this union was to produce other human beings. It was part of God's plan and instruction to Adam and Eve: "And God blessed them. And God said to them, 'Be fruitful and multiply and fill the earth and subdue it'" (Gen. 1:28). Adam and Eve had sex and produced children: "Now Adam knew Eve his wife, and she conceived and bore Cain, saying, 'I have gotten a man with the help of the LORD.' And again, she bore his brother Abel" (Gen. 4:1–2). Propagation was a part of the plan and purpose of marriage. God didn't tell us that children will suffer when they are born outside of marriage; he just gave us marriage and said to have children within this union. We have sadly come to know how detrimental it is to man, woman, and child when children are born and reared in broken homes, in divorced families, and with absentee fathers and mothers. Being married doesn't mean you have to have children. But in marriage is where children are to be born.

Conversion—The Charge of Marriage

The amazing God of heaven designed the world and equipped humanity to carry out the purposes of his will. Chief among them are teaching, training, and educating the next generation. The most important subject for any human to learn is God. The expectation is simple—Adam and Eve were to teach their children about the God who made them. Their children, in turn, were to teach their children and so on and so on.

By the time Israel became a nation and was delivered from Egyptian bondage, God told Moses to call the whole nation together and give them this charge.

> Hear, O Israel: The LORD our God, the LORD is one. You shall love the LORD your God with all your heart and with all your soul and with all your might. And these words that I command you today shall be on your heart. You shall teach them diligently to your children,

and shall talk of them when you sit in your house, and
when you walk by the way, and when you lie down, and
when you rise. You shall bind them as a sign on your
hand, and they shall be as frontlets between your eyes.
You shall write them on the doorposts of your house
and on your gates...And when the LORD your God
brings you into the land that he swore to your fathers,
to Abraham, to Isaac, and to Jacob, to give you—with
great and good cities that you did not build, and houses
full of all good things that you did not fill, and cisterns
that you did not dig, and vineyards and olive trees that
you did not plant—and when you eat and are full, then
take care lest you forget the LORD, who brought you
out of the land of Egypt, out of the house of slavery.

—Deuteronomy 6:4–12

Marriage is two people sharing their lives together. Blessed with children, those people are commanded to teach their children about the
great God who made them and loves them. Those who will be married must have this thought in mind about their children. No one else
is supposed to teach your children about God; you are. This makes
sense when you consider they are yours; no one on earth loves them
more; and you have them for most of the time in their lives. By design, children spend more time with their parents than anyone else.

Timothy is a great example of a person who was reared in a home
where God was taught. Paul said of him, "I am reminded of your sin-
cere faith, a faith that dwelt first in your grandmother Lois and your
mother Eunice and now, I am sure, dwells in you as well" (2 Tim. 1:5).

Notice a few more powerful passages teaching this truth, (emphasis added ELO)

For I know him, that *he will command his children and his
household after him, and they shall keep the way of the LORD,*

to do justice and judgment; that the LORD may bring upon Abraham that which he hath spoken of him.

—Genesis 18:19 KJV

Now therefore fear the LORD, and serve him in sincerity and in truth: and put away the gods which your fathers served on the other side of the flood, and in Egypt; and serve ye the LORD. And if it seem evil unto you to serve the LORD, choose you this day whom ye will serve; whether the gods which your fathers served that were on the other side of the flood, or the gods of the Amorites, in whose land ye dwell: but *as for me and my house, we will serve the LORD.*

—Joshua 24:14–15 KJV

Fathers, do not provoke your children to anger, *but bring them up in the discipline and instruction of the Lord.*

—Ephesians 6:4, ESV

Children are not simply cute, cuddly little play partners to dress up and pose for lots of pictures. Rather, they are human beings with eternal souls. If you are an adult, you were once a baby, and what happened is you grew. When parents have children, they often think about their growth, but it is typically physical growth. We think about their health, so we feed them healthy things and make sure we take them to the doctor. We think about their education, so we teach them, take them to school, and may even start a college fund for them.

But not enough parents think about their souls. Your marriage is the place where humans are produced and where souls either learn to live with God or without God. Fix this in your mind, every soul must live somewhere eternally. Our homes will largely determine whether our children spend eternity in heaven or hell. When you think about your children, think about their souls.

Civility—Life's Lesson Plan

Every human being comes from other human beings. God's design is that those who produce us will teach us. Adults should know how to act largely because they were taught but also because they have lived and learned. Those people owe it to their children to teach them how to behave.

Our parents are our primary teachers; they should teach us about manners. When we are born, we don't know how to talk; we only know how to cry. Our parents teach us to say "please" when we request things and "thank you" when we receive them. We should consider marriage as our own little nation. The parents are in charge of training and disciplining; the children are the students and citizens of the nation.

When they go outside of the home and into society, the training they received should lead to civility. Children who board buses for a ride to school should know how to behave and follow instructions when they arrive at the bus stop. When the same child reaches the classroom, the teacher should be able to teach math, not manners.

Failure at home leads to failure in society; after all, society is made of people from homes. Our homes and the marriages that produce children are where children are to learn how to live in society. When children enter the world, the parents who bore them are to teach them how to live in that world.

One of the terrible events in scripture is when Ammon, the son of David, raped his half-sister, Tamar. She pled with him not to force her. The appeal she made was to his training at home. The thing he was attempting should not have been done in Israel. Nothing he had learned at home should have led him to think this action was proper. He would be a fool, and she would be ashamed.

> She answered him, "No my brother, do not violate me,
> for such a thing is not done in Israel; do not do this

outrageous thing. As for me, where could I carry my shame? And as for you, you would be as one of the outrageous fools in Israel. Now therefore, please speak to the king, for he will not withhold me from you." But he would not listen to her, and being stronger than she, he violated her and lay with her.

—2 Samuel 13:12–14

All of us are the products of not merely biology but also of our environments and influences. The marriage that produces children is charged with teaching those children how to live civil lives. If we don't learn how to act at home, we will be challenged to know how to live in society.

Fidelity to God—A Reason to Marry
Humanity has not changed since creation; men and women see an attractive person, and not surprisingly, we are attracted. But God has designed sex to be enjoyed inside of marriage, and for many, God's design creates a problem. In answering questions about marriage, Paul wrote some very practical things for the church in Corinth and for us:

Now concerning the matters about which you wrote: "It is good for a man not to have sexual relations with a woman." But because of the temptation to sexual immorality, each man should have his own wife and each woman her own husband.

—1 Corinthians 7:1–2

Having sex without being married is sinful. Scripture calls it fornication (Eph. 5:3). The solution is to get married and then have sex with your spouse. Of course, having sex is not the only reason to get married. Getting married expressly for sex is not a very good idea because marriage involves so much more than just having sex. Sex should be viewed as one of the blessings of the relationship, but *it is the relationship that is truly important.*

First Corinthians 7:9 says, "But if they cannot exercise self-control, they should marry. For it is better to marry than to burn with passion." God made us sexual beings; the desire to be with someone is natural. He also calls upon us to exercise self-control and be faithful to him if we are not married. If we have to choose fidelity to God or fornication, we should get married and avoid fornication. Faithfulness to God is one more reason he designed marriage.

Sexual Enjoyment—A Blessing from God
Sex is a great blessing for humanity given to us by God. It is not dirty and in marriage should never be viewed with shame. Sex manifests God's love for us it is without doubt one of the closest and most intimate moments a man and a woman can ever share.

It is sad beyond description that this great joy has been so cheapened by humanity. We have taken the relationship, commitment, and meaning out of sex and replaced them with quick, meaningless physical gratification. This is how we have reached the point of having one-night stands and no-name hook-up sex. Our culture is stripping all of the beauty and significance God intended for sex down to body parts and secretions.

God made us and gave us the joy of sex, and he intended for us to enjoy it inside of marriage. The marriage is to be held in honor, and the marital bed should be undefiled (Heb. 13:4). In marriage, each person is free to explore each other sexually. God has placed no limitations on the things a married couple can do with each other sexually. Sex is for the enjoyment of each person. The wife is not the husband's sex slave; neither should she view sex as a duty that she forces herself to fulfill.

Sex is to be mutually meaningful and satisfying to both parties:

> The husband should give to his wife her conjugal rights, and likewise the wife to her husband. For the

wife does not have authority over her own body, but the husband does. Likewise the husband does not have authority over his own body, but the wife does. Do not deprive one another, except perhaps by agreement for a limited time, that you may devote yourselves to prayer; but then come together again, so that Satan may not tempt you because of your lack of self-control.

—1 Corinthians 7:3–5

"Good girls" are sometimes challenged in marriage by the things their husbands request or they themselves want to try. They should not worry about this because no one is as good as God, and he gave us sex. Sex should be seen as a blessing and enjoyed in marriage, where God intended it. Sex is not the most important thing in marriage, but it is important and should be seen as such. Sex is not when the wife services her husband. It is when a husband and wife share intimate moments of closeness and connection in marriage.

Modeling—Emulate God
God reveals himself to us in relationships that we can understand. When Jesus taught the disciples to pray, he told them to approach God as their Father (Matt. 6:9). By association and understanding, we are to think of God as our parent. Because we become fathers and mothers, we really come to know how much God loves us.

This is the point that Jesus tried to convey to his audience as he spoke of God's goodness. To get them to understand it, he used their goodness toward their children.

Ask, and it will be given to you; seek, and you will find; knock, and it will be opened to you. For everyone who asks receives, and the one who seeks finds, and to the one who knocks it will be opened. Or which one of you, if his son asks him for bread, will

give him a stone? Or if he asks for a fish, will give him
a serpent? If you then, who are evil, know how to give
good gifts to your children, how much more will your
Father who is in heaven give good things to those who
ask him?

—Matthew 7:7–10

Since children are to be had by those who are married, then marriage becomes a way to model God. When we become parents, the best
course of action is to parent our children the way God parents us.

Revelation of the Mystery—The Model of Marriage
The point of scripture is that God through Christ will redeem us
from sin back to himself (2 Cor. 5:18–19). The imagery used to por-
tray this great event and God's wonderful love is marriage:

Therefore a man shall leave his father and mother and
hold fast to his wife, and the two shall become one
flesh. This mystery is profound, and I am saying that it
refers to Christ and the church.

—Ephesians 5:31–32

How is a husband to love his wife? Answer: as Christ loved the church.
How is a wife to submit to her husband? Answer: as the church submits to Christ. Paul teaches us how we are to behave toward one another by revealing how Christ loved the church. In marriage, the
husband fills the place of Christ, and the wife stands in the stead of
the church.

It would be wonderful for us to realize before we leap into marriage that it is reflective of the mystery of God. Consider the importance of God's work in bringing the church into existence (Eph.
1:1–13). Paul tells us that each member of the Godhead played a part

in bringing our redemption. The Father promised; Christ perfected through his blood; and the Holy Spirit revealed God's Word and sealed us. What a different way to think about marriage.

Protection—A Powerful Provision

Whether or not marriages produce children, the people within a family are assured of the protection of being a member of the family. Children should be safe at home because their parents should protect them from harm. Women should be safe at home because their husbands should protect them from harm.

This dynamic is a provision provided by marriage. A good demonstration of this is seen when Levi and Simeon (sons of Jacob) heard the news that their sister Dinah had been violated. The individual who did it asked to marry her, and the men responded with deceit. Read the passages and listen to their explanation for their behavior.

> And all who went out of the gate of his city listened to Hamor and his son Shechem, and every male was circumcised, all who went out of the gate of his city. On the third day, when they were sore, two of the sons of Jacob, Simeon and Levi, Dinah's brothers, took their swords and came against the city while it felt secure and killed all the males. They killed Hamor and his son Shechem with the sword and took Dinah out of Shechem's house and went away. The sons of Jacob came upon the slain and plundered the city, because they had defiled their sister. They took their flocks and their herds, their donkeys, and whatever was in the city and in the field. All their wealth, all their little ones and their wives, all that was in the houses, they captured and plundered. Then Jacob said to Simeon and Levi, "You have brought trouble on me by making me stink to the inhabitants of the land, the Canaanites and the Perizzites. My numbers are few, and if they

gather themselves against me and attack me, I shall be destroyed, both I and my household." But they said, "Should he treat our sister like a prostitute?"

Genesis 34:24–31

Absalom was another man who sought to protect and avenge his sister (2 Sam. 13:1–39). There is a lot of uncertainty and danger in the world. If a person breaks into someone's home and puts a person's family at risk, no one will begrudge the person who protects his family by stopping the threat. Marriages afford protection to those involved and their family, and this is by design.

Empathy—Connection With God
Having children allows us to connect to God in a different way than not having them. There may be no greater human love than the love parents have for their children. As we rear them, we grow to understand patience, long suffering, and love. The need to repeat ourselves becomes an expected part of the job. So when God calls us his children, we can really identify with what he means (1 John 3:1–2). How much do you love your children? Now, how much does God love his?

The only rival to the love parents have for children is the love spouses have for one another. This love may actually trump the love of children because this love is what provided for the children. This is the love where vows were taken and life was pledged, and in this we can really understand and empathize with God.

God gave an entire book in the Bible to help us see how he feels. The prophet Hosea was told by God to go marry a woman and their relationship would be the illustration of how God's people had treated their marriage to him:

The word of the LORD that came to Hosea, the son of Beeri, in the days of Uzziah, Jotham, Ahaz, and

Hezekiah, kings of Judah, and in the days of Jeroboam the son of Joash, king of Israel. When the LORD first spoke through Hosea, the LORD said to Hosea, "Go, take to yourself a wife of whoredom and have children of whoredom, *for the land commits great whoredom by forsaking the LORD.*" *(emphasis added ELO)*

—Hosea 1:1–2

Hosea's wife was unfaithful to him and even had children by another man. She then left the marriage and became a prostitute. She came back defiled, used, and abused, and God told Hosea to go and buy her back. The man had to go buy his wife from her pimp, and he did.

And the LORD said to me, "Go again, love a woman who is loved by another man and is an adulteress, even as the LORD loves the children of Israel, though they turn to other gods and love cakes of raisins." So I bought her for fifteen shekels of silver and a homer and a lethech of barley. And I said to her, "You must dwell as mine for many days. You shall not play the whore, or belong to another man; so will I also be to you." For the children of Israel shall dwell many days without king or prince, without sacrifice or pillar, without ephod or household gods.

—Hosea 3:1–4

How would you feel if your spouse behaved like Gomer? Because of marriage, we know how God feels when we are unfaithful to him. Marriage could be the single greatest relationship to understand how God thinks about, feels about, and behaves toward his people. If you have never felt sorry for God, then you have never considered that God is married to his people; if you are married, marriage enables you to empathize with God.

Our alien guest asked us what marriage was, and we began to describe it. What did you write for your description? How about your spouse and children? In 1988, I would have done well to ask myself not what I wanted to get out of marriage but rather, what did God intend when he gave us marriage.

Let us make sure we tell those coming behind us what marriage is from God *before* they go to the beach, I mean altar.

Marriage—A Definition

A divine institution ordained by God comprised of one man (male) and one woman (female) in which each joins (glues) himself to the other until death parts them. It supersedes all other earthly relationships; it imitates God's relationship with ancient Israel and Christ's relationship with his New Testament church. It is the origin of the home and family and the place for childbearing and rearing.

3

GOD'S DESIGN FOR MARRIAGE: DESIGN DETERMINES FUNCTION

Our alien guest would undoubtedly have more questions, and we will seek to help him understand. He now knows what marriage is, but he would not know how it is intended to function. The male and female would certainly interest him, and he would want to know more. To help him understand function, we might begin by describing design.

According to dictionary.com, the word *design* is defined as:

1. a plan or drawing produced to show the look and function or workings of a building, garment, or other object before it is built or made.
   synonyms: plan, blueprint, drawing, sketch, outline, map, plot, diagram, draft, representation, scheme, model
2. purpose, planning, or intention that exists or is thought to exist behind an action, fact, or material object.

God Is a God of Design
The God of heaven is a God of design; things work the way they do because God designed them to work the way they do. The world was

created in six days; the first five were to prepare for the arrival of man. The prophet Isaiah says as much:

> "I made the earth and created man on it; it was my hands that stretched out the heavens, and I commanded all their host."...For thus says the LORD, who created the heavens (he is God!), who formed the earth and made it (he established it; he did not create it empty, he formed it to be inhabited!): "I am the LORD, and there is no other."
>
> —Isaiah 45:12, 18

The world is governed by laws established by God—gravity, sowing and reaping, and planet alignment and rotation are just a few of those laws. Humans are also designed—our minds and bodies are no accident. With this David agrees:

> I praise you, for I am fearfully and wonderfully made. Wonderful are your works; my soul knows it very well. My frame was not hidden from you, when I was being made in secret, intricately woven in the depths of the earth. Your eyes saw my unformed substance; in your book were written, every one of them, the days that were formed for me, when as yet there was none of them.
>
> —Psalm 139:14–16

The wise Proverb writer wrote, "The hearing ear and the seeing eye, the LORD has made them both" (Prov. 20:12).

God designed the world and created humanity to live in the world he created. It is reasonable to believe that when he created marriage, he also did so with design. The design shows the look and function or workings; design shows purpose, planning, or intention behind an action, fact, or object.

What Is God's Design for Marriage?

In simple terms, and we will certainly say more, in marriage God designed for the man to lead his wife and family. Scripture will use the phrase "the husband is the head of the wife." With this design our culture certainly disagrees. If we get the design wrong, the function will fail. Things don't work as they should when people ignore or change the design of the creator. A hammer is great for driving nails, but hammers are terrible for slicing bread. Design determines function.

- If we get the design wrong, marriage won't function as intended by the designer.
- The function is determined by the design.
- The design comes from the purpose and thought of the designer.

- We will fight against God.

God's Design (Gen. 2:18–25)

Genesis 2:18 reads, "It is not good that the man should be alone." This is simply what it says; the design of that fact follows. Design—"I will make him a helper fit for him." We will talk about this in more detail later in the book.

Genesis 2:19–20 explains the thought of the designer. Of the animals present before Adam, nothing was fit for him:

> Now out of the ground the LORD God had formed every beast of the field and every bird of the heavens and brought them to the man to see what he would call them. And whatever the man called every living creature, that was its name. The man gave names to all livestock and to

the birds of the heavens and to every beast of the field. But for Adam there was not found a helper fit for him.

The creation of woman was designed because nothing else was fit for the man. Genesis 2:21 tells us what God did about the situation.

So the LORD God caused a deep sleep to fall upon the man, and while he slept took one of his ribs and closed up its place with flesh. And the rib that the LORD God had taken from the man he made into a woman and brought her to the man.

Genesis 2:23 provides us with Adam's reaction to and recognition of God's design. Adam said, "This at last is bone of my bones and flesh of my flesh." As contrasted with what? Not another woman. Adam didn't go to e-Harmony.com, match.com, or ChristianMingle.com to find his soul mate. Neither did he sort through a hundred dates and find "the one." Please read the Bible: he had the animal kingdom pass before him, and he named them. He saw them and realized there was nothing in all of those like him. God made a woman, and when Adam saw her, he said, "This at last is bone of my bones and flesh of my flesh."

In Genesis 2:24, God instructs Adam about what this means. "Therefore shall a man leave his father and his mother and hold fast to his wife, and they shall become one flesh."

How Do You Get That the Husband Is the Head of the Wife out of That?

This is a great question and one for which we need more scripture. It is established in Genesis 2, and it is explained elsewhere. Every time the roles of husbands and wives are mentioned in the Bible, the husband is always the head of his wife, and this is never reversed. The wife is never the head of the husband. Consider the following passages.

To the woman he said, "I will surely multiply your pain in childbearing; in pain you shall bring forth children. Your desire shall be for your husband, and he shall rule over you."

—Genesis 3:16

But I want you to understand that the head of every man is Christ, the head of a wife is her husband, and the head of Christ is God.

—1 Corinthians 11:3

For the husband is the head of the wife even as Christ is the head of the church, his body, and is himself its Savior.

—Ephesians 5:23

I do not permit a woman to teach or to exercise authority over a man; rather, she is to remain quiet. For Adam was formed first, then Eve.

—1 Timothy 2:12–13

This is a sampling of passages, but they all teach the same thing, and Paul says this design is due to the fact that Adam was formed first. The world, humanity, and marriage were all designed by God; each is to function in a particular way. The function of marriage is that the husband is the head of the wife. Genesis 2 is the creation of marriage and if we disagree with God's design from the beginning how can our marriages function the way he intended.

For Some, God's Design Is Unpalatable

Sadly, men rebelled against God's design and took advantage of their position even abusing women. This abuse gave rise to feminism and radical feminism. According to Wikipedia the word *feminism* is defined as the advocacy of women's rights on the grounds of political, social, and economic equality to men. Given this definition, nothing I say should be construed as disagreeing with that. Women are created in God's image, and they are equal to men in every way before God. However, pay close attention to the definition of *radical feminism,* according to Wikipedia.

> Radical feminism is a philosophy emphasizing the patriarchal roots of inequality between men and women, or, more specifically, social dominance of women by men. Radical feminism views patriarchy as dividing rights, privileges and power primarily by gender, and as a result oppressing women and privileging men. Radical feminists tend to be more militant in their approach (radical as "getting to the root").

> Radical feminism opposes existing political and social organization in general because it is inherently tied to patriarchy. Thus, radical feminists tend to be skeptical of political action within the current system, and instead support cultural change that undermines patriarchy and associated hierarchical structures.

> Radical feminism opposes patriarchy, not men. To equate radical feminism to man-hating is to assume that patriarchy and men are inseparable, philosophically and politically.

It is not my desire or intention to discuss philosophical and political issues. But the relationship of husband and wife is patriarchal, and this is precisely the point of Genesis 2:18–25. God made Adam first, and God placed Adam over Eve; this is the design of the relationship. Male leadership is from God, not men.

Adam didn't create himself and then Eve; God did. Adam didn't decide he would be made first and by so doing he would be Eve's head; God did. In marriage, radical feminism's disagreement is with God, not man. And men and women who side with radical feminism must oppose God's design for a husband to be the head of his wife.

Did God Explain How His Design Was to Function?

Adam Was to Lead; Eve Was to Follow

After their creation and marriage, Adam and Eve sinned against God. The result was their eyes were opened; they knew that they were naked, and they hid themselves. What happens next is demonstrative of God's design of male leadership. In Genesis 3:6, it is clear that Eve ate of the fruit of the tree first. After she ate, she gave the fruit to Adam, and he ate.

Even though she ate first when God approached them, notice where and with whom he began.

> And they heard the sound of the LORD God walking in the garden in the cool of the day, and the man and his wife hid themselves from the presence of the LORD God among the trees of the garden. But the LORD God called to the man and said to him, "Where are you?" And he said, "I heard the sound of you in the garden, and I was afraid, because I was naked, and I hid myself." He said, "Who told you that you were naked? Have you eaten of the tree of which I commanded you not to eat?" The man said, "The woman whom you gave to be with me, she gave me fruit of the tree, and I ate."

> —Genesis 3:8–12

Because God approached Adam first this indicated that Adam was the head.

Whenever a problem exists, we go to the person who is in charge. The leader is the one who is to answer for what went wrong under his or her charge. After speaking to Adam, God did talk to Eve next, and she was punished for her own action. You may think that it is a stretch to suggest that just because God talked to Adam first, that meant he was in charge. Such a thought is dispelled when you hear God talk to Adam the second time.

> And to Adam he said, "Because you have listened to the voice of your wife and have eaten of the tree of which I commanded you, 'You shall not eat of it,' cursed is the ground because of you; in pain you shall eat of it all the days of your life; thorns and thistles it shall bring forth for you; and you shall eat the plants of the field. By the sweat of your face you shall eat bread, till you return to the ground, for out of it you were taken; for you are dust, and to dust you shall return."
>
> —Genesis 3:17–19

Scripture even attributes the first sin to Adam (Rom. 5:12). God was not pleased that Adam listened to his wife instead of listening to him. Eve led Adam, but he was supposed to lead her. For those who disagree, this is a point they must admit. Someone is going to lead; there is no such thing as a leaderless home. Either Eve leads Adam, or Adam leads Eve. Female leadership is not the way God designed marriage.

Before we leave this point, also consider what Paul said to Timothy regarding how he was to behave in the church (1 Tim. 3:14–15). In 1 Timothy chapter two, Paul describes the roles of men and women and uses Adam and Eve as an example:

> I do not permit a woman to teach or to exercise author-
> ity over a man; rather, she is to remain quiet. For Adam
> was formed first, then Eve; and Adam was not deceived,
> but the woman was deceived and became a transgressor.
>
> —1 Timothy 2:12–14

She can't exercise authority or rule over him because Adam was formed first. That truth is not cultural it is creational. The husband is to lead his wife; they can't both lead.

Leadership Was in the Design

God never intended to arrange dual leaders or co-leaders. The issue was that the man was alone, and God said that it was not good. Then God said he was going to make a helper "fit for him." Remember when God said that nothing else was fit for Adam? Only the woman, a female, is fit for the man. The King James Version says of this verse, "I will make a help meet for him." The woman is fit; she is meet for the man.

God never said, "It is not good that the man should be alone. I will make him a *help lead*." This is a modern assumption, not a biblical doctrine. She was a help meet, not a help lead.

God Explained His Design Ultimately in Christ (Ephesians 5:22–32)

For those who disagree with male leadership, Ephesians 5 will be a challenging text to explain because, in it, Paul uses marriage to illustrate Christ's love and provisions for his church. The husband occupies the place of Christ in the marriage, and the wife occupies the place of the church. The scriptural emphasis is that Christ is the head of the church, and Christ leads the church. The church is subject to Christ, and the church follows Christ. No one would suggest that the church helps Christ lead or that the church does not submit to Christ. Certainly, it wouldn't be thought that the church leads Christ or that Christ is subject to his church.

The Words God Used to Convey His Design for Husband and Wife
These verses cannot be read and explained any other way than that
God designed for husbands to lead their wives.

> To the woman he said, "I will surely multiply your pain in
> childbearing; in pain you shall bring forth children. Your
> desire shall be for your husband, and *he shall rule over you.*"

—Genesis 3:16

> But I want you to understand that the head of every
> man is Christ, *the head of a wife is her husband,* and the
> head of Christ is God. For man was not made from
> woman, but woman from man. Neither was man cre-
> ated for woman, but woman for man.

—1 Corinthians 11:3; 8–9

> Wives, submit to your own husbands, as to the Lord.
> For *the husband is the head of the wife even as Christ is the
> head of the church,* his body, and is himself its Savior.
> Now as the church submits to Christ, so also *wives
> should submit in everything to their husbands.*

—Ephesians 5:22–24

> Let a woman learn quietly with all submissiveness. *I
> do not permit a woman to teach or to exercise authority over
> a man;* rather, she is to remain quiet. For Adam was
> formed first, then Eve; and Adam was not deceived, but
> the woman was deceived and became a transgressor.

—1 Timothy 2:11–14

Older women likewise are to be reverent in behavior, not slanderers or slaves to much wine. They are to teach what is good, and so train the young women to love their husbands and children, to be self-controlled, pure, working at home, kind, *and submissive to their own husbands,* that the word of God may not be reviled.

—Titus 2:3–5

Likewise, wives, *be subject to your own husbands,* so that even if some do not obey the word, they may be won without a word by the conduct of their wives, when they see your respectful and pure conduct. Do not let your adorning be external—the braiding of hair and the putting on of gold jewelry, or the clothing you wear—but let your adorning be the hidden person of the heart with the imperishable beauty of a gentle and quiet spirit, which in God's sight is very precious. For this is how the holy women who hoped in God used to adorn themselves, *by submitting to their own husbands, as Sarah obeyed Abraham,* calling him lord. And you are her children, if you do good and do not fear anything that is frightening.

—1 Peter 3:1–6

The design of the designer determines the function of the thing designed. Design is the purpose, planning, or intention that exists or is thought to exist behind an action, fact, or material object.

Our world has taken an aggressive posture against God's design. It has replaced male leadership with female leadership or some hybrid of the two—or, for some, no leadership at all. This is not God's design, and it is part of the problems we are experiencing in our marriages. It could be argued that we have seen what giving men this kind of power over women has produced in the past and in many instances still does.

Man's abuse of women cannot be disputed. But, saying that God designed male leadership is not synonymous with saying that males lead as God designed. This chapter has sought to establish God's design and intent. I'm not saying men lead as God intended—quite the contrary. Men did and do abuse their position and act terribly inconsistent with God's intention. It is wrong for any man to abuse his wife. This will be echoed frequently in this book.

However, the fact that people abuse things designed for certain functions doesn't remove the design. Men did go astray, and they do today; this does not destroy God's design, and we are not at liberty to throw out the baby with the bath water. The world has rejected God's design, and many in the church seem bent on doing the same thing.

We cannot have the marriages we desire and God intended by rejecting or changing the design of the designer who gave it to us. According to the Bible, God's design for marriage is that the husband is the head of his wife. Cultural disagreement does not change God's word.

4

APPLYING GOD'S DESIGN
BEYOND MARRIAGE

I t might help us appreciate God's design in marriage if we saw God's design in other areas of life. For, God has not limited his design of one person being over another person to marriage. The design is seen in every type of relationship we have. Seeing the design in other areas will help us understand it in marriage. Human wisdom believes that God's way is wrong and that male leadership in marriage is the source of marital difficulties. So in our wisdom, we have set aside God's way and installed ours. This is actually what has led to our problems, and it is this that I am writing against.

This chapter consists largely of verses that demonstrate through various examples the design of God. The next chapter will take the point made here and apply it to marriage. Remember, God appointed people to lead other people. The one appointed was placed in that position by God. Marriage is appointed by God; he placed men as the heads of their wives. We will discuss *how* a man is to lead later–see his section. The point we are making here is that he is *supposed* to lead. Consider these examples, and see how they relate to the design of marriage.

Moses and Aaron

> So Moses and Aaron said to all the people of Israel,
> "At evening you shall know that it was the LORD
> who brought you out of the land of Egypt, and in
> the morning you shall see the glory of the LORD,
> because he has heard your grumbling against the
> LORD. For what are we, that you grumble against
> us?" And Moses said, "When the LORD gives you in
> the evening meat to eat and in the morning bread
> to the full, because the LORD has heard your grum-
> bling that you grumble against him—what are we?
> Your grumbling is not against us but against the
> LORD."
>
> —Exodus 16:6–8

Moses point to Israel was he and Aaron were nothing. God heard
their grumbling and they murmured against him. Your grumbling is
not against us but against the Lord.

David and Saul

> Then said Abishai to David, "God has given your enemy
> into your hand this day. Now please let me pin him to
> the earth with one stroke of the spear, and I will not
> strike him twice." But David said to Abishai, "Do not
> destroy him, for who can put out his hand against the
> LORD's anointed and be guiltless?" And David said, "As
> the LORD lives, the LORD will strike him, or his day
> will come to die, or he will go down into battle and per-
> ish. The LORD forbid that I should put out my hand

against the LORD's anointed. But take now the spear that is at his head and the jar of water, and let us go."

—1 Samuel 26:8–11

David understood that Saul was God's anointed therefore he would not lift his hand against him.

Elders to Members

Take heed therefore unto yourselves, and to all the flock, over which the Holy Ghost hath made you overseers, to feed the church of God, which he hath purchased with his own blood.

—Acts 20:28

Obey your leaders and submit to them, for they are keeping watch over your souls, as those who will have to give an account. Let them do this with joy and not with groaning, for that would be of no advantage to you.

—Hebrews 13:17

Shepherd the flock of God that is among you, exercising oversight, not under compulsion, but willingly, as God would have you; not for shameful gain, but eagerly.

—1 Peter 5:2

Members must submit to, follow and obey elders because God designed this role.

Government to Citizens

Let every person be subject to the governing authorities. For there is no authority except from God, and those that exist have been instituted by God. Therefore whoever resists the authorities resists what God has appointed, and those who resist will incur judgment. For rulers are not a terror to good conduct, but to bad. Would you have no fear of the one who is in authority? Then do what is good, and you will receive his approval, for he is God's servant for your good. But if you do wrong, be afraid, for he does not bear the sword in vain. For he is the servant of God, an avenger who carries out God's wrath on the wrongdoer. Therefore one must be in subjection, not only to avoid God's wrath but also for the sake of conscience. For because of this you also pay taxes, for the authorities are ministers of God, attending to this very thing. Pay to all what is owed to them: taxes to whom taxes are owed, revenue to whom revenue is owed, respect to whom respect is owed, honor to whom honor is owed.

—Romans 13:1–7

Scripture is always clear that Christians must be good citizens because God ordained government. Unless the government demands that God's people disobey God, Christians must submit.

Masters to Servants (Bosses to Employees)

Servants, be obedient to them that are *your* masters according to the flesh, with fear and trembling, in singleness of your heart, as unto Christ; Not with eye service, as men pleasers; but as the servants of Christ, doing the will of God from the heart; With good will doing service, as to the Lord, and not to men.

—Ephesians 6:5–7 KJV

Servants, be subject to your masters with all fear; not only to the good and gentle, but also to the forward.

—1 Peter 2:18 KJV

Parents to Children

Children, obey your parents in the Lord: for this is right. Honor your father and mother" (this is the first commandment with a promise;) That it may go well with you, and that you may live long in the land.

—Ephesians 6:1–3

Children, obey your parents in everything, for this pleases the Lord.

—Colossians 3:20

Husbands to Wives
For the husband is the head of the wife, even as Christ is the head of the church, his body, and is himself its Savior. Now as the church submits to Christ, so also wives should submit in everything to their husbands.

—Ephesians 5:23–24

The Point of the Chapter

Reading the Bible is hardly a problem for anyone; applying the Bible can create a challenge for everyone. Every relationship we have is covered by this design—civic, career, familial, and religious. The design is simple, in every instance, someone is over someone else. When it comes to husbands and wives, many people want the design to stop. It can't stop there; marriage was the first place the design was established and revealed (Gen. 2:18–25).

Remember that we are trying to establish God's design, not defend men's behavior. I am disputing our cultures rejection of male leadership in marriage. And their offered solution of no leadership, joint leadership, or female leadership. If our marriages are having problems, it is because we are not following God's design and Christ's example. Changing, rejecting, or substituting God's design for ours has proven to be of no help at all. When will we learn that we cannot improve on what God has designed?

5

FLAG ON THE PLAY—
YOU'VE GONE TOO FAR

"**M**uch learning has made you mad." At least when Paul was so accused, he did have much learning. Personally, I suffer from no such delusion. Have I gone too far? For some, I'm sure I have. It may be argued that the husband/wife relationship is not the same as the others listed in the previous chapter. A woman's husband is not her ruler like Moses was to Israel. He is not the government and she his citizen, nor is he an elder and she the member.

Neither is the husband the parent, and the wife the child. She is not any of these things—with that I certainly agree. A woman's husband is none of these things to her, and that was not the point of the last chapter; neither is it the point of this one.

He is not the boss and she his employee or servant though some men and women may think that is what I'm saying. This could even be misunderstood by children. I read a joke some time ago that a father was showing his young child their wedding photos. He talked about the ceremony, the commitment, and the love he and his wife shared. He came to the picture of his wife and said, "Here's Mommy in her wedding dress. See how beautiful she was?" Then the child asked, "Daddy was that the day Mommy came to work for us?"

While he is none of those things to her, what he is in her life is in the same position. His role in his wife's life has the same authority as the others. The designer designed marriage to function under the same premise. That premise is simple—someone is over someone else or representative leadership.

Try applying our cultures position of no one is over anyone or no male leadership in marriage to all the other areas of God's design.

Someone Is over Someone Else

Israel to Moses

If Moses was our leader today he might hear, "Moses, you are not over us. What you need to understand is that if we are happy, then you will be happy. Or, Moses, you better make sure you've got your stuff together before we will follow you"? Israel tried this and it did not work well for them.

Citizens to Government

The president of the United States is often referred to as the leader of the free world. We don't refuse to follow the president or tell him that, as citizens, we will help him lead or we will tell him how to lead. Even when we don't agree with the person or policies we submit to the position.

Members to Elders

Men govern their homes, but they are under the oversight of an eldership. Members are not allowed by God to refuse to follow elders. We would think it strange if members told elders, "We don't have to follow you; or we are not under you, nor are you over us." All members understand that we are under the oversight of the elders.

Employees to Bosses

No one would encourage employees to tell their bosses, "I don't have to listen to you," or "You had better treat me right first, then I'll show up on time." "By the way, boss, I was watching the clock, and I saw you come in late three times, and until you get your act together, I'll be late as well." Such an attitude and action will likely result in termination.

Parents to Children
There are few, if any, people in the world who enjoy disrespectful, disobedient children. Children shouldn't tell their parents, "I will if you will. If you want to be happy, make me happy. Then we will all get along."

The Principal of Representative Leadership Seems to Work Everywhere but in Marriage
In Scripture the same language is used to describe all of these relationships, and yet in marriage, a drastic change has occurred. The world in opposition to God has told women to throw off male leadership in their marriages.

Question: When did God change his mind about his design? And why does the same design work in every relationship, while being rejected in marriage?

Consider these biblical statements: "*Your desire shall be to your husband and he shall rule over you*"; "*Wives, submit yourselves to your own husbands as to the Lord*"; "*Let the older women teach the younger women to obey their husbands*"; "*And you wives see that you reverence your husband*"; "*For Adam was first formed then Eve.*"

How did these and all other biblical instructions that place a husband over his wife get reduced to "If Mama ain't happy, nobody's happy?" or "Happy wife, happy life," or "The man is the head, but the woman is the neck." When did it become good advice for older men to tell a young man engaged to be married to just learn these two responses: "Yes, dear," or "I'm sorry." I have heard such advice given with my own ears. Men are asked, often by other men, "Do you want to be right, or do you want to be happy?"

Now we hear statements like these from some women concerning their husbands. He knows he'll be in the doghouse. If he misbehaves, he'll sleep on the couch. He knows what will happen. He listens to me; I don't listen to him. Some women are saying these things and they mean them. Older women tell younger women, girl, you don't really have to listen to your husband; just let him believe he is in charge.

DO YOU TAKE GOD?

Where did anyone ever read any of this in the Bible? Who told us that it was all right to add these things or change what we do read?

Few wives these days have any reverence for their husbands. For many the word reverence has become a dirty word. Little children are honest; some say, "My mom doesn't listen to my dad; he listens to her," or "My mother wears the pants in our house." This is what makes the idea of no one leading so misleading. We didn't think men were doing a good enough job, so we just replaced them with women.

He Has The Last Say

The world says we are equal partners, there are no roles. While the church has accommodated the world but hedging by changing *rule over* and *obey* to, "You have a say, but he has the last word." First of all, thank you for allowing men to have the last word, human wisdom is more than kind. But, second, let me tell you what that actually means. It simply means he has a say, then she has a say, and after her say, he gets to say her say last. The last word is his privilege to say her word last.

The sad part is that many men have capitulated under the influence of the world and say the same things. Men who stand next to their wives and listen to them tell others how many children she has—and he is included in the number—are nothing if not a disgrace and shame to the Almighty. These men are not even co-regents. They are children. How far have we gone from Adam being first formed to hearing men introduced as children by their wives?

Such a sick, sad departure from God's design hurts everybody involved. No woman referring to her husband as one of her children is happy about it. She married him to be a leader, especially if she planned to follow God. How disappointing for her to be pregnant with his child and have to rear him as well. It hurts her, it hurts him and it hurts the children, it overburdens the wife, emasculates the husband and confuses the children. Wow, that is a long way from Genesis 2.

The Problem Is That Many Women Are Taught Wrong

Too many women are taught radical feminism. They are taught that male leadership is the problem and must be cast off. At the same time boys are taught they are to be weak and soft, almost feminine. Boys are also taught to never think of themselves as a leader, because that would be rude. When the subject of being a husband is taught to boys they are taught that they will grow up to be big strong oafs, who don't know much and from whom not much is expected. Their taught that being an intelligent, assertive, confident man is synonymous with being arrogant, rude and unfeeling. This is because boys are also taught by radical feminist.

Girls grow up hearing, "You are a queen; he is lucky to have you. You know he doesn't know what he is doing. He is in need of help, and you are just the one to help him. You can't put your trust in a man. You have a say, girl; you need to be heard. Speak your mind." The messages that are designed to strengthen women often have the secondary affect of denigrating men.

These messages embolden women to doubt, distrust, and reject male leadership before they ever enter marriage. Foolish advice is given by foolish women, and young women and old come to the marriage with the wrong thought in mind. When bad advice is given and followed bad things happen.

For all of the independent women running their homes how is that working for you? For all of the men who have been relegated to a figurehead leader, a toothless lion how is that working for you?Houses are being built and torn down by the occupants themselves. Wisdom encourages a woman to build her house. Every wise woman builds her house, but the foolish woman tears it down with her own hands (Prov. 14:1). Doctrines, ideologies and philosophies that are contrary to God if followed will ruin our marriages. And we are seeing the fruit of following the world's wisdom.

Historically, Women Were Abused

Because of the abuses of men, women are now repulsed by a man being over them. No one enjoys being mistreated and abused. History records many atrocities perpetrated on a wide range of individuals and groups.

Women Are No Different

Women's suffrage was real because women were suffering; no one can dispute the ill treatment women have received, and in many places of the world continue to receive, from men. However, the answer is not what has happened in our marriages. We have replaced male leadership with female leadership.

The biblical concept of the husband being over the wife has become a myth or folklore—so much so that the biblical concept is not even understood by either party as they enter marriage. Unfortunately, little in a young lady's life will ever give her the truth about the design God has for marriage. Generations of young people in our culture have been indoctrinated to believe that what God designed denigrates women, exalts men and is to be avoided at all cost. So much so that after hearing God's design taught, some women will literally say, "I don't understand that can you explain it again."

Following is how to understand it.

How to Understand a Personal Truth

So whatever you wish that others would do to you, do also to them.

—Matthew 7:12

Whenever we need to understand how to treat one another, Matthew 7:12 is the verse to help us. It teaches us an undeniable truth, no one wants to be mistreated. When people can't seem to understand how black people can still talk about slavery and still be bothered by the past from time to time, I wonder if they can understand the feelings of the colonists toward England. Should someone of European descent bring up the ill treatment perpetuated by England, would anyone understand how they could still be bothered? Patrick Henry wanted liberty or death; if one can understand this, one can understand black people's issue with slavery.

I wonder if such people can understand the feelings of the Jews today toward Hitler. If a person who was a descendant of the persecuted Jews spoke about the Holocaust today, would anyone have any problem understanding how he could still feel that way? What about the feelings of one of Native-American descendant speaking about the Trail of Tears today? Could anyone understand it?

The point is this: if you can understand the principle in one area, you can understand it in others.

The Same Is True for Women

Some women either don't want to or refuse to understand the principle of male leadership in their home as God designed it. In order to understand it simply apply the very thing we just discussed; these women can understand the principle of leadership when they are the leader. Every mother understands her authority over her children? She may respond but I'm not his child, of course you aren't. But in the relationship you are over your child and this is what you are being asked to understand.

She also understands her authority as a boss. Every woman who manages others clearly understands her role. She is over her employees and as such they should submit, listen and follow her leadership. The nature of the relationship is understood by everyone when we are in charge. In marriage God designed the man to be the head of his wife. If you can understand it as a parent or when you are the boss then you can understand it in marriage.

How Did We Get Here?

Whenever we lose our way, this is a good question to ask ourselves. How did we get here? The answer is known and is simple to state. Dare I say it again, men abused women, and women finally overcame some of the abuse. Whenever abuse occurs and those who were under it overcome, a pattern emerges, and we see it now in marriage.

1. The abused cry out and ask for it to stop (this usually falls on deaf ears).
2. The abused bring grievances and begin seeking equality, using force if necessary.
3. With success, they arrange things legally to ensure that the abuse is never resumed.
4. In accomplishing number three, the abused becomes the abuser.

The way to ensure that the abuse will not resume is to invite the abused to help establish new guidelines going forward.

Colonists went from taxation without representation to manifest destiny. They were not even a nation and then they became "God's nation." Homosexuals, though never subjected to the same abuse from the government as others. Have come out of the closet and gone to the Supreme Court. Now they are trying to silence all critics and sue everyone who disagrees—even to the point of a mayor seeking to examine the content of local preachers' sermons.

This Is What Has Happened With Women in Marriage

Saying that a man is over a woman is now anathema. If one says it in public, he could be tarred and feathered. If not, he is simply laughed at and scorned. Sadly, it is not even believed by people who claim to believe the Bible. "That was then," they say. "No one really believes that anymore and Paul was speaking out of cultural ignorance." Silly, me I thought he was inspired of God (2 Tim. 3:16-17). He believed the things he preached were the commandments of the Lord (1 Cor. 14:37).

Even in "conservative churches," nothing will fill an auditorium with a silence so loud as to be deafening than saying the husband is the head of the wife. The few who preach it are hailed as bold for doing so. Those who listen meet him at the back and say with a wry smile, "Preacher, you'd better be careful." Still others jokingly say, "Boy, you may not make it out of here, preaching like that."

All of this nonsense is precisely why the problems persist. No man should ever abuse, mistreat, or lord his role over his wife. The abuse perpetuated by husbands coupled with our self-will has now moved us to reject God's Word altogether. The world has influenced the church so much that preachers and elders are saying that there are no such roles, and they bend over backward to avoid saying it and will turn the scriptures into pretzels to avoid teaching it.

Everyone Gets It but You

I can't count the times I've been told that. But, it certainly seems true on this subject. I'm the one behind the times and failing to understand. I suppose so, but when I say what they tell me is the truth, no one seems to like hearing it. I suppose, like everyone else, I should accept the fact that women rule. Who runs the world - girls!

Should we all just say it together that women have become the rulers of their homes? Men are simply figureheads. They have the appearance of being in charge, but everyone knows she is. Let's change the saying "behind every good man is a good woman." Maybe "beside every good man is a good woman," but why stop there?

In most homes today, it's "behind every good woman is a man...I mean, child." Is this the position that the world wants me to get? No worries a bunch of us men have gotten it. Men have learned well to just say, "Yes, dear" "Ask your mom" or "Honey I was waiting to for you to tell me?"

I'm glad we can all agree that the problem is not an inability to understand someone leading someone else. The real problem is who that someone is. If the woman leads the man, it is all right. But, if the man is said to lead the woman well, that is a problem. I think I read that arrangement in Genesis 3:6, and apparently God didn't approve of the woman leading.

So sorry...as it turns out, I don't get it, because God didn't design the wife to lead; in fact he spoke against it (Gen. 3:17).

She Has Her Say

Says who? Women have their say, their voice; they demand to be heard, and men must listen. What does that look like in a typical marriage? I'm glad you asked.

The man and woman enter into marriage with both understanding that she has her say, but he has the last word. Both assured and convinced that men cannot lead and that women are more capable. Both are also convinced that leadership from a man to a woman is mean and rude. Within this context a woman "having her say" is not the good thing the world thinks it is.

Once married, the man has some ideas and shares them with his wife. She listens to what he has to say, and then she offers her say. This seems innocent enough, but as the marriage goes on, a pattern emerges. Everything he says becomes open for discussion, even when he did not intend for a discussion to ensue. Because she has her say, it never dawns on her that there are times when he was informing her, not asking her. She sees nothing wrong, because her say is expected and accepted. Believing it is her right and duty to help lead, she listens to his say and then qualifies it with her say.

In her mind, she believes that this is how marriage works it is how a husband and wife with no roles of leadership direct their family. So whenever he comes to her with a decision, she listens then sets forth her reasons for or against, and off they go. The man, wanting to make his wife happy and because older men told him to just learn to say "yes, dear," he does. Remember, that they asked him, "Do you want to be happy or right?" They told him, "It's your fault, even when it isn't your fault. Just apologize." And an assertive, intelligent man is rude so he follows the instruction given.

Over time, her say becomes the counter to his say. He offers up something; she examines it and ponders whether it is a good idea or not. If she does not think so, she shares her opinion and tells him why his idea won't work. Sometimes it doesn't take him coming up with an idea; her say becomes the first say, and he gets to say her say last.

This process becomes the norm, he brings things to her or he listens to her. In time, he becomes accustomed to the process and as men do, he seeks to reduce the steps in the process, you know smarter not harder. He does this because he now knows that in the end his decisions must be vetted through his wife, he simply starts asking her, "What do you think we should do about this or that?" By now, he is largely out of the business of making decisions—or originating ideas, that job now belongs almost exclusively to his wife's. Her word becomes what they do, and his word decreases. Now she is the leader.

Under this new arrangement it takes the family awhile to learn that women don't lead the same as men lead. Women tend to multitask more than men, this can be a counter productive quality especially in leading a family. Women who lead their families move quicker and more quickly from item to item than men. Men tend to be slower and more methodical, which quality is often a bother to their wives.

Soon hers is the only voice heard in the house, and it is heard often. Things don't change as quickly as her mind works, and it is frustrating. Children are difficult, and the more she tries, the harder it seems to be to get them to respond to her instructions. To exert her authority, she raises her voice believing this will help her get her point across more effectively. Unlike her husband, who seems bothered by nothing, everything seems to bother her, and she can't seem to fix any of it to her liking.

She and the children talk a lot, but their attention spans are about as short as her patience have grown with them. They will not listen and do what they are told. Their attitudes stink; they are unappreciative and disrespectful. And if all of that is not bad enough, she cannot get her husband to support her. The children listen to him but not to her, and he won't tell them to listen to her. He is distant, unresponsive and appears uninterested in helping her. While she is overworked, stressed out and frustrated in a way that almost defies words.

Did You Miss It?
A shift has taken place in the home. The disdain for male leadership has given rise to female leadership. In far too many marriages, the above scenario is the norm. Males are supposed to lead, and they don't know what to do when they don't, so many of them do nothing. A lot of men have become like furniture, it makes the place comfortable, its nice but mostly, it just sits there.

Many men have abdicated the role of leadership and are now distant, quiet, unresponsive spectators in their homes. She won't say it, but he is just about good for nothing to her. He has largely become just like one more of her children, which is why some women actually say it. Unfortunately for her, he still wants sex on demand. Of course to him, it might be the only time he gets an opportunity to lead.

God's design is true; he made them male and female. He made him to lead. When he is not leading, he is not doing what he is made to do. Many wives are disappointed that their husbands won't support them, and many husbands know they are not supposed to. It should be the other way around, but it's not. In the typical home, the husband has become her support. Sadly, he has become a *help unsuitable* for her!

What About The Children?

The husband's role has devolved into mere support of his wife's message. Unfortunately for him, he doesn't always agree with what she says. But he is not the leader, he has a new role. He has become the mediator between two warring factions. The children come to him for help. When they see him alone, they catch him to talk to him about Mom. "Dad, you know she's being unreasonable; you know she's being unfair. Dad," they plead, "do something."

He hears the babies he loves and looks into their eyes, and he knows. He knows Mom is too demanding sometimes. She asked the child to make life changes on Monday, and it is now Tuesday at 6:00 p.m. What the child is waiting on is anyone's guess. He also knows that he has failed them—he has not led; he has caved. He gave in to his own insecurities, to the world's pressure, and to human wisdom. And now he spends his time refereeing, not leading. He often hears himself ask his children to be mature adults and help make Mom's life easier. What he really is asking his children is to help make his life easier so that he is less of a disappointment to his wife.

And when his wife catches him alone, she also begs for help. She pleads with him to support her and stand up for her. She implores him to be a man before the children. He nods sheepishly and agrees that something needs to be done. He assures his wife, "I know you're right," then he agrees to talk to the children.

What he knows is he has failed his wife. Instead of being a man to the children, he should be a man to his wife. Instead of supporting her, he should encourage her to follow him. He ought to have a plan to lead, but he doesn't. The ship has sailed, and now he believes he can't get it back to shore. So he is stuck trying to satisfy his wife and children while disappointing both—and his God. Here is a question, where is God in all of this? Where is God in most marriages?

God Is Not Pleased When His Design Is Rejected
The Bible gives us several examples of God designating someone to lead. Scripture also records instances of people attempting to change God's design. It also records God's reactions. Moses's own brother and sister are a good example. Apparently, they thought Moses was getting too much press, and they wanted everyone to know they had a say as well. They spoke against Moses, and God spoke against them.

Aaron and Miriam—Numbers 12:1–9

> Miriam and Aaron spoke against Moses because of the Cushite woman whom he had married, for he had married a Cushite woman. And they said, "Has the LORD indeed spoken only through Moses? Has he not spoken through us also?" And the LORD heard it. Now the man Moses was very meek, more than all people who were on the face of the earth. And suddenly the LORD said to Moses and to Aaron and Miriam, "Come out, you three, to the tent of meeting." And the three of them came out.
>
> And the LORD came down in a pillar of cloud and stood at the entrance of the tent and called Aaron and Miriam, and they both came forward.

And he said, "Hear my words: If there is a prophet among you, I the LORD make myself known to him in a vision; I speak with him in a dream. Not so with my servant Moses. He is faithful in all my house. With him I speak mouth to mouth, clearly, and not in riddles, and he beholds the form of the LORD. Why then were you not afraid to speak against my servant Moses?" And the anger of the LORD was kindled against them, and he departed.

God asked a very sobering question we should all consider. Why was Miriam and Aaron not afraid to speak against God's design. Why aren't we? God chose Moses to lead Israel and God chose men to lead their wives and families.

God plagued Miriam with leprosy, and she was unclean for seven days for this rebellion. Aaron cried to Moses, and Moses cried to God. It did not take everyone involved long to realize that a huge error in judgment had been made. Numbers 12:10–15 continues the account:

When the cloud removed from over the tent, behold, Miriam was leprous, like snow. And Aaron turned toward Miriam, and behold, she was leprous. And Aaron said to Moses, "Oh, my lord, do not punish us because we have done foolishly and have sinned. Let her not be as one dead, whose flesh is half eaten away when he comes out of his mother's womb." And Moses cried to the LORD, "O God, please heal her—please." But the LORD said to Moses, "If her father had but spit in her face, should she not be shamed seven days? Let her be shut outside the camp seven days, and after that she may be brought in again." So Miriam was shut outside the camp seven days, and the people did not set out on the march till Miriam was brought in again.

How serious was God about his design for Moses to lead Israel? When he gave Miriam leprosy, she was going to die. The disease would have certainly killed her if God had not healed her. She would have been separated from everyone else for having it, and she would have endured a slow, painful death. God is not pleased when his design is rejected.

Korah, Dathan, and Abiram—Numbers 16:1–50

These three men were priests, but that was not enough for them. They wanted Aaron's job. They led a revolt against Moses and Aaron and gathered quite a following. Their accusation was much the same as Aaron's and Miriam's. They thought Moses and Aaron had taken too much power upon themselves. Moses pled with them not to rebel against God. He assured them that just being priests was special and should be enough.

A test was undertaken with everyone bringing his censer to see who God would approve. God approved of Aaron, and the situation resulted in many deaths in Israel. Consider some of the things said from those involved.

Korah

> Now Korah...took men. And they rose up before Moses, with a number of the people of Israel, 250 chiefs of the congregation, chosen from the assembly, well-known men. They assembled themselves together against Moses and against Aaron and said to them, "You have gone too far! For all in the congregation are holy, every one of them, and the LORD is among them. Why then do you exalt yourselves above the assembly of the LORD?"
>
> —Numbers 16:1–3

Moses

And Moses said to Korah, "Hear now, you sons of Levi: is it too small a thing for you that the God of Israel has separated you from the congregation of Israel, to bring you near to himself, to do service in the tabernacle of the LORD and to stand before the congregation to minister to them, and that he has brought you near him, and all your brothers the sons of Levi with you? And would you seek the priesthood also? Therefore it is against the LORD that you and all your company have gathered together. What is Aaron that you grumble against him?"

—Numbers 16:8–11

God

And the LORD spoke to Moses and to Aaron, saying, "Separate yourselves from among this congregation, that I may consume them in a moment." And they fell on their faces and said, "O God, the God of the spirits of all flesh, shall one man sin, and will you be angry with all the congregation?" And the LORD spoke to Moses, saying, "Say to the congregation, Get away from the dwelling of Korah, Dathan, and Abiram."

—Numbers 16:20–24

God's displeasure with this rebellion culminated in the deaths of these men and those who followed them. The earth opened and swallowed them, and this rebellion in Israel was put down.

And Moses said, "Hereby you shall know that the LORD has sent me to do all these works, and that it has not been of my own accord. If these men die as all men die, or if they are visited by the fate of all mankind, then the LORD has not sent me. But if the LORD creates something new, and the ground opens its mouth and swallows them up with all that belongs to them, and they go down alive into Sheol, then you shall know that these men have despised the LORD."

And as soon as he had finished speaking all these words, the ground under them split apart. And the earth opened its mouth and swallowed them up, with their households and all the people who belonged to Korah and all their goods. So they and all that belonged to them went down alive into Sheol, and the earth closed over them, and they perished from the midst of the assembly.

And all Israel who were around them fled at their cry, for they said, "Lest the earth swallow us up!" And fire came out from the LORD and consumed the 250 men offering the incense.

—Numbers 16:28–35

Representative leadership is God's design, and those who lead do so with God's approval. When that leadership is rejected as being wrong, replaced with something different, or repudiated as evil, that action is taken against God. Moses didn't declare himself Israel's leader, because he wasn't. God was their leader, and Moses was God's representative; therefore, refusing to follow Moses was refusing to follow God (Heb. 10:28-31). Men and women must come back to this understanding in marriage and parenting.

I can't emphasize enough that nothing is here said about how well a man leads. The point is that according to God's design, he is *supposed* to lead. If we set aside God's Word in this area, God's Word will also be set aside when God tells him *how* to lead. The God who demands that you love your wife as Christ loved the church also demands that you lead your wife as Christ leads the church.

God made man. God made woman. God made marriage. Marriage will work best when the design of the designer is followed.

6

NO ONE HAS THE RIGHT
TO SIN AGAINST GOD

Because we have not followed God's design many husbands and wives have hurt each other. Before we address his or her section a discussion of sin is in order. Because when we sin against each other, we often overlook that we are also sinning against God. Being wronged is a terrible thing. It hurts, it causes confusion, and it disrupts our relationships. Interestingly, the closer the people are to us, the more severely they are able to hurt us.

It is precisely our love for them that makes the pain we feel so intense when wronged by them. This is why being wronged by our spouses is so confusing. Among the many questions we ask ourselves and them is why. "Why would someone I love with all of my heart and who claims to love me with all of his/her heart hurt me so badly?" It's a good question, but we rarely get a satisfactory answer.

Our solution to our pain is often to retaliate and inflict our own pain in return. This is not the answer and proves only to cause more harm. If we ever hope to heal, we must begin with our relationship with God, not our relationship with each other. There are several reasons for looking to God. One reason is if we focus on our relationship with each other, we will both assure ourselves that we are the injured party. Even if we did wrong first, we will be angry because we apologized and then watched as our spouse did us wrong in return.

We will go around in circles blaming each other and both feeling justified as we hold on to our proof of the other person's wrongdoing.

Beginning with God instead will provide the best and proper perspective for our relationships. Our relationship with God is to be the example and blueprint we use to engage in relationships with others. It forces us to look beyond ourselves. It also forces us to admit that God never did anything wrong to us; we did wrong to him. This admission is critical for successful relationships for it softens our hearts and opens us up to acknowledge our wrongs without focusing on someone else's. Neither one of us has the right to sin against God.

The proper perspective, then, is always *upward, inward,* and then *outward.* Consider the vision of Isaiah; notice what he saw and what he said.

In the year that King Uzziah died I saw the Lord sitting upon a throne high and lifted up; and the train of his robe filled the temple. Above him stood the seraphim. Each had six wings with two he covered his face, and with two he covered his feet, and with two he flew. And one called to another and said: Holy, holy, holy, is the Lord of hosts; the whole earth is full of his glory! And the foundations of the thresholds shook at the voice of him who called, and the house was filled with smoke. And I said: Woe is me! For I am lost, for I am a man of unclean lips, and I dwell in the midst of a people of unclean lips; for my eyes have seen the King, the Lord of hosts!

—Isaiah 6:1–5

Looking *upward* Isaiah saw the king in his glory, he was overwhelmed by what he saw. He also heard "holy, holy, holy," and he knew the earth was full of the glory of the Lord. His view of God turned his view *inward.* In God's presence—and maybe for the first time in his life—he could see himself clearly. He was lost, and he was unclean, and he knew it. In view of seeing God and himself, he then turned *outward* and could see others clearly. He was unclean, and he was in the midst of a people of unclean lips. He explained why he drew this conclusion: "for my eyes have seen the King, the Lord of hosts." This passage powerfully helps us understand what we and others look like before God.

Before we judge others for doing us wrong, we must see ourselves in the presence of God because we have wronged him. David also understood this well. After seeing God and himself clearly, he made this profound admission to God. He said,

> For I know my transgressions, and my sin is ever before me. Against you, you only, have I sinned and done what is evil in our sight, so that you may be justified in your words and blameless in your judgment.
>
> —Psalm 51:3–4

The major reason we have such a hard time forgiving others who wrong us is because we count people sinning against us greater and more important than our sinning against God.

When we can see God clearly and see ourselves clearly, we can then clearly see the need for and develop the desire to forgive others, for we are all unclean people who dwell in the midst of unclean people. Let's remind ourselves of how bad our sins are and ask God to forgive us. Then he can strengthen us to forgive others.

Second Samuel 11:22–27 recounts a low point in David's life. If we can relate, we can forgive.

> So the messenger went and came and told David all that Joab had sent him to tell. The messenger said to David, "The men gained an advantage over us and came out against us in the field, but we drove them back to the entrance of the gate. Then the archers shot at your servants from the wall. Some of the

king's servants are dead, and your servant Uriah the Hittite is dead also." David said to the messenger, "Thus shall you say to Joab, 'Do not let this matter displease you, for the sword devours now one and now another. Strengthen your attack against the city and overthrow it.' And encourage him." When the wife of Uriah heard that Uriah her husband was dead, she lamented over her husband. And when the mourning was over, David sent and brought her to his house, and she became his wife and bore him a son. But the thing that David had done displeased the LORD.

David sinned he actually committed several sins throughout this event. But we dare not isolate and rate sins as if ours is lighter or better than someone else's. Sin is the transgression of God's law (1 John 3:4). When we sin we act contrary to God, we go beyond his law and we live for ourselves. We yield to the lust of the flesh, the lust of the eyes or the pride of life (1 John 2:15-16). No matter what is done to us neither one of us has the right to sin against God.

In reading about sin in the Bible one is drawn to a court scene. Sin is committed, it is against God as such you need an advocate or legal representation. The sinner will be judged by law and will be punished. The conclusion about sin then is that it is a spiritual crime worthy of the death penalty (Rom. 6:23). All sin is always against God, following are a few.

Lying	Drunkenness	Homosexuality	Indecency
Cheating	Greed	Divisions	Malice
Stealing	Swindlers	Dissensions	Envy
Fornication	False witness	Covetousness	Cursing
Murder	Sowing discord	Unfaithfulness	Idolatry
Gossiping	Jealousy	Lust	Materialism

Hate	Laziness	Orgies	Unforgiving
Adultery	Ungodliness	Disobedience to parents	

There is one word for all of these things, and that word is *sin*. The list is hardly exhaustive; for others, read Romans 1:18–32; 1 Corinthians 6:9–11; Galatians 5:19–21, and Revelation 21:8. Even those lists are not all-encompassing, so Galatians 5 has the summary phrase "and such like." It is important for us all to stop ignoring, minimizing, or intentionally neglecting the fact that our sin is against God. Looking at how offensive our sins are to God will help us put others who sin against us into perspective.

Why Sin Is Offensive to God

Sin Is Selfish

> And the LORD sent Nathan unto David. And he came unto him, and said unto him, There were two men in one city; the one rich, and the other poor. The rich man had exceeding many flocks and herds: But the poor man had nothing, save one little ewe lamb, which he had bought and nourished up: and it grew up together with him, and with his children; it did eat of his own meat, and drank of his own cup, and lay in his bosom, and was unto him as a daughter.

> —2 Samuel 12:1–3

Sin Is Self-Serving

> And there came a traveler unto the rich man, and he spared to take of his own flock and of his own herd.

> —2 Samuel 12:4

Sin Disregards Others

But the poor man had nothing, save one little ewe lamb...[and] the rich man...took the poor man's lamb, and dressed it for the man that was come to him.

—2 Samuel 12:3–4

Sin Deserves Death

And David's anger was greatly kindled against the man; and he said to Nathan, As the LORD liveth, the man that hath done this thing shall surely die: And he shall restore the lamb fourfold, because he did this thing, and because he had no pity.

—2 Samuel 12:5–6

Sin Manifest Ungratefulness

And I gave thee thy master's house, and thy master's wives into thy bosom, and gave thee the house of Israel and of Judah; and if that had been too little, I would moreover have given unto thee such and such things.

—2 Samuel 12:8

Sin Despises God's Commands

Wherefore hast thou despised the commandment of the LORD.

—2 Samuel 12:9

Sin Is Evil

Wherefore hast thou despised the commandment of the LORD, to do evil in his sight? thou hast killed Uriah the Hittite with the sword, and hast taken his wife to be thy wife, and hast slain him with the sword of the children of Ammon.

—2 Samuel 12:9

Sin Will Be Punished

Now therefore the sword shall never depart from thine house...Thus saith the LORD, Behold, I will raise up evil against thee out of thine own house, and I will take thy wives before thine eyes, and give them unto thy neighbour, and he shall lie with thy wives in the sight of this sun.

—2 Samuel 12:10–11

And it came to pass on the seventh day, that the child died. And the servants of David feared to tell him that the child was dead: for they said, Behold, while the child was yet alive, we spake unto him, and he would not hearken unto our voice: how will he then vex himself, if we tell him that the child is dead?

—2 Samuel 12:18

Sin Despises God

Now therefore the sword shall never depart from thine house; because thou hast despised me, and hast taken the wife of Uriah the Hittite to be thy wife.

—2 Samuel 12:10

Sin Disrespects God's Presence

For thou didst it secretly: but I will do this thing before all Israel, and before the sun.

—2 Samuel 12:12

Whither shall I go from thy spirit? or whither shall I flee from thy presence?...If I say, Surely the darkness shall cover me; even the night shall be light about me. Yea, the darkness hideth not from thee; but the night shineth as the day: the darkness and the light are both alike to thee.

—Psalm 139:7, 11–12

Sin Steals from Others

He spared to take of his own flock and of his own herd, to dress for the wayfaring man that was come unto him; but took the poor man's lamb, and dressed it for the man that was come to him.

—2 Samuel 12:4

Thou hast killed Uriah the Hittite with the sword, and hast taken his wife to be thy wife, and hast slain him with the sword of the children of Ammon.

—2 Samuel 12:9

Sin Is a Personal Attack on God

Wherefore hast thou despised the commandment of the LORD.

—2 Samuel 12:9

Now therefore the sword shall never depart from thine house; because thou hast despised me.

—2 Samuel 12:10

And David said unto Nathan, I have sinned against the LORD.

—2 Samuel 12:13

Sin Empowers God's Enemies

Howbeit, because by this deed thou hast given great occasion to the enemies of the LORD to blaspheme, the child also that is born unto thee shall surely die.

—2 Samuel 12:14

Sin Sent Jesus to the Cross

And as they were eating, Jesus took bread, and blessed it, and brake it, and gave it to the disciples, and said, Take, eat; this is my body. And he took the cup, and gave thanks, and gave it to them, saying, Drink ye all of it; For this is my blood of the new testament, which is shed for many for the remission of sins.

—Matthew 26:26–28

Acknowledge That All Sin Is against God

Have mercy on me, O God, according to your steadfast love; according to your abundant mercy blot out my transgressions. Wash me thoroughly from my iniquity, and cleanse me from my sin! For I know my transgressions, and my sin is ever before me. Against you, you only, have I sinned and done what is evil in your sight, so that you may be justified in your words and blameless in your judgment.

—Psalm 51:1–4

How long has it been since you consciously thought about your sin against God? Everything listed above about sin is what we have done to God. David lusted, committed adultery, got a man drunk, lied, deceived, covered up, conspired, murdered, and then married the wife of the man he had killed. David was selfish: he stole, despised God, ignored God, and gave the enemies of God opportunity to blaspheme. David did all of this against God. David was the man, and so are you, and so am I.

We must not think only of our sins against others and theirs against us. If we do, we will develop a point value and a system of comparison for sin. Of course, we will be the one who establishes which sin gets the most points. And we will be the one to compare ourselves to others.

When we do this, is it really surprising that we tend to think of ourselves as better than others? With such thinking, our sin is never quite as bad as the sins of others. Our sins never quite rise to the same level of disgust. It goes without saying that our sins never cause quite the same amount of pain or harm. And our sins always need to be understood in light of one who is growing and making mistakes along the way to maturity. We would never sin intentionally like those evil people who keep sinning against us.

This is the start of all sorts of other bad thoughts and actions. This thought leads us to believe that our spouses' sins against us are worse than our sins against them—*if* we are even calling our actions sin; our deeds might simply be mistakes. Or they might be justified because of all we have put up with from our spouse. Additionally, your spouses' refusal to admit that their wrongs are worse than yours serves as one more proof of how bad off they really are.

But what if your spouse is doing the same thing to you that you are doing to them, do you think that your offenses are lower or higher on their scale? They are certain of the exact same thing you are certain of—that you are worse sinner than they are. An in entire chapter is dedicated to learning to forgive like God. Refusing to forgive each other contributes to our problems. In many instances we refuse to forgive and instead we blame and accuse each other while excusing ourselves. If we blame each other, while excusing ourselves is it any wonder our marriages suffer.

Question: *are husbands and wives counting their sins against God?*

When we sin, we all sin against God, and we should never justify ourselves because we are "not as bad" as our spouse. Your spouse is not the standard; God is. Our sin against God is why Jesus came to die; your sin and mine sent Jesus to the cross. Never forget that; always be willing to admit that. When we acknowledge our sin, cry over our sin, fall before God, and ask for mercy, then we can better deal with our spouse's sin against us.

Failure in this area is why we struggle to forgive each other. Our struggle to forgive may not be due to the great injury we've endured. It may be due to the great amount of pride we have about our own sin against God. Maybe this is the reason we are holding on to things from the past and can't seem to let them go. Do you really believe that your spouse's sin against you is worse than your sin against God? Your actions reflect your belief.

Consider this—refusing to forgive others is also sinning against God (Matt. 6:14–15). How long have you been sinning against God by refusing to forgive those who've wronged you? What if God took that approach with you? He said he would. If you don't forgive men their trespasses, your father in heaven won't forgive you, your trespasses. This includes your spouse.

We can learn to forgive others when:

1. We acknowledge our own sin against God.
2. We admit to God and ourselves how offensive sin is to God.
3. We are willing to accept the sentence from God due to sin.
4. We thank God for forgiving our sin against him.
5. We are willing to emulate God's actions toward us to others.

Sin ruins, destroys and ends marriages. Are your sins against God destroying your marriage? Let's ask him to forgive us for sinning against him. Then we can allow his forgiveness of us to motivate us to forgive one another.

Design determines function, God designed men to lead their families. How men are to lead is determined by Christ the next section discusses Christ as the model husband. May all husbands commit to love and lead their wives as Christ loves and leads the church.

SECTION 2

Chapters 7-11

Christ A Husband's Example in Marriage

For Him

7

HEAVEN PRESENTS: WOMAN

When we are asked to reconsider a thing like marriage, it is helpful to go back to familiar things and look at them anew. I've read Genesis 2 many times, but in writing this material, I went back and read it again with a fresh perspective. I'd ask you to do the same.

I've been talking about the world's disagreement with God's order and design. Because men abused women, women rejected male leadership. In so doing, society rejected God's design. Many men have acknowledged their failure and agreed with women. These men accept the conclusion that women should have a try at leading. It has not worked, and we are experiencing many troubles in our marriages as a result.

The reason is simple—the world disagrees with God. The world influences us; we then find ourselves in agreement with the world and at odds with God. Our friendship with the world puts us at enmity with God. Those who oppose God never win; their ways prosper temporarily at best.

Our homes are suffering, families are hurting, and marriages are troubled because of the world's influence. Individuals are saddened, and their faith is hindered. For many, the number-one hurdle to their faithfulness to God and happiness in life is their marriage! How sad is that? I'm not talking about an individual's actions within the confines of marriage.

There is right and there is wrong, and men and women do both in marriage. I'm not trying to pinpoint who is to blame and what has gone wrong in your marriage. I am asking you what did God intend when he gave us marriage. Are you and your spouse living that out, or have you changed God's design? Let's go back to the beginning so we can move forward in our marriages by taking a closer look at Genesis 2.

A Home, a Job, and Then a Wife—Genesis 2:15–17

.

What Was God's Design for Adam?

Everyone desires a fair and honest hearing; why not give God one? Genesis 1 records the creation of the world. Genesis 2 provides us with more detail about some of those events. The creation of man and woman is given more detail in chapter 2, and so is marriage.

What Did God Do? Genesis 2:15

The Lord God took the man and put him into the garden of Eden to work it and keep it. The words *dress* and *keep* (KJV) or *work* and *tend* (ESV) are defined below. Brown Driver and Briggs e.sword.com says of these words:

The word *work*:

1) to work, serve
   1a 1) to labor, work, do work
   1a 2) to work for another, serve another by labor

The word *work* is also used in these other passages: Genesis 2:5; 3:23; 4:2; 4:12. Abel was a keeper of sheep; Cain was a worker of the ground.

The word *keep*:

1) to keep, guard, observe, give heed
   1a 1) to keep, have charge of
   1a 2) to keep, guard, keep watch and ward, protect, save life

To see other passages where this word is used, consider that when Adam and Eve were put out of the garden, the angel kept or guarded the tree of life (Gen. 3:24; 4:9; 24:6).

God's Intention for Adam

In considering Adam, an older man told me many years ago, "Adam had a home, a job, and then God gave him a wife." God gave Adam a command. Man has always been under the authority of God. Adam also has a relationship with God, and God's desire for him was to be obedient.

What Did God Say?

> And the LORD God commanded the man, saying, "You may surely eat of every tree of the garden, but of the tree of the knowledge of good and evil you shall not eat, for in the day that you eat of it you shall surely die"
>
> —Genesis 2:16–17

A Problem Solved— Genesis 2:18–25

> And the Lord God said, It is not good that the man should be alone; I will make him an help meet for him. And out of the ground the Lord God formed every beast of the field, and every fowl of the air; and brought them unto Adam to see what he would call them: and whatsoever Adam called every living creature, that was the name thereof. And Adam gave names to all cattle, and to the fowl of the air, and to every beast of the field; but for Adam there was not found an help meet for him. And the Lord God caused a deep sleep to fall upon Adam, and he slept: and he took one of his ribs, and closed up the flesh instead thereof; And the rib, which the Lord God had taken from man, made he

a woman, and brought her unto the man. And Adam said, This is now bone of my bones, and flesh of my flesh: she shall be called Woman, because she was taken out of Man. Therefore shall a man leave his father and his mother, and shall cleave unto his wife: and they shall be one flesh. And they were both naked, the man and his wife, and were not ashamed (KJV).

Read it for yourself, and you will agree that the entire scene is about Adam. From the beginning, this notion should be understood: male emphasis = male expectation. Genesis 2 by the numbers:

References to Adam (twenty-four times)

1. Adam = six times: 19, 20, 21, 23
2. Man = six times: 18, 22, 23, 24, 25
3. Him = three times: 18, 20
4. His = five times: 21, 24, 25
5. He = two times: 19, 21
6. My = two times: 23

References to Eve (seven times)

1. Her = one time: 22
2. Woman = two times: 22, 23
2. She = two times: 23
3. Wife = two times: 24, 25

All references to her connect her to Adam.

Observations and Considerations for Those Who Lead
First, God said, "It is not good that the man should be alone." The actions taken are God's doing. The personal pronouns can't be missed.

1. "I will make him [for him] one suitable."
2. Luke 3:38 says, "Adam was the son of God."
3. Eve was God's answer to his son's aloneness.

Second, God made Eve from Adam.

1. God put him to sleep.
2. From his side, he made a woman.
3. She is part of him.
4. She is from inside of him.

Third, she was brought to him. This pattern needs to be understood.

1. God made her *for* the man. "*I will make a help meet for him.*"
2. God made her *from* the man. "*The rib he took from the man made he a woman.*"
3. God brought her *to* the man. "*And brought her unto the man.*"
4. This is God's doing, not man's.

God's Actions Should Teach Us

God observed that his son had a problem. Everyone who is a father can understand that. Adam's father moved to solve his problem. His son didn't have to ask for help; in fact, he might not have even known that he needed it. The father provided the best possible answer for his son. Every father would do the same. If his son has a problem, he would use his resources to help him.

If God is your father, and he is going to help solve your problem, he would also use his resources. The great thing about God is that he is infinite in power, might, and wisdom. We can conclude the following from God's actions in the garden:

1. Woman is special—there is nothing in existence like her.
2. Woman is equal—no one else was suitable.

3. Woman is presented—there was no other for him.
4. Woman is connected—there was no other from him.
5. Woman is spiritual—she is the only other one made in the image of God.
6. God made her *for* him, *from* him, and brought her *to him*!

When Adam saw Eve for the first time and spoke about what he saw, his speech tells us plainly that he understood God's intention, and he was thankful. His words express devotion to the one God made. His proclamation shows the uniqueness and closeness to Eve that God intended. Adam also manifested an understanding of the unity he shared with Eve.

1. His speech shows understanding: "This is now!"
2. His speech expresses devotion: "Bone of my bones..."
3. His speech expresses uniqueness: "Flesh of my flesh."
4. His speech expresses unity: "She will be called woman."

The Hebrew words for man and woman are closely connected; we can't say "woman" without saying "man" (*ishsha*—woman, *ish*—man) [Strong's concordance e-sword.com].

Later, when Adam was throwing Eve under the bus, he did so to God with this acknowledgment: "The woman whom you gave to be with me, she gave me fruit of the tree, and I ate" (Gen. 3:12). Most naturally, it reads like Adam is blaming Eve. I did hear of one person who thought Adam was defending his actions. Instead of blaming her, he was asking God, "Since you gave her to be with me, what else could I do? She ate and gave it to me. I couldn't be apart from her, so I ate."

I think he was trying to save himself by blaming her. But the thought is a nice one. Everyone in the garden knew that Eve was made for Adam, and God was the one who did the giving.

Application

She Is Heavenly

All women (wives) are unique, important, and special by the design of God. Adam (man) did not create or cause this. Adam merely recognized it the very first time he saw Eve. Every woman needs to know that she is special as well as the reason she is. That reason is this: she is special, unique, and important because she is made in the image of God.

> Then God said, "Let us make man in our image, after our likeness. And let them have dominion over the fish of the sea and over the birds of the heavens and over the livestock and over all the earth and over every creeping thing that creeps on the earth." So God created man in his own image, in the image of God he created him; *male and female he created them.*"
>
> —Genesis 1:26–27

Her importance is not because of her creativity, looks, feelings, or anything physical. She is not special because, as I heard one woman say, "After God made man, he took one look and said, 'I know I can do better.' Then he made a woman." She is not better than a man, certainly she is not worse. There was nothing lacking in Adam; neither was there anything lacking in Eve. Both were perfect just as God designed them. Both were perfectly suitable for the roles he created for them.

God made Eve special; God made her unique; God made her important. She shares God's image, which makes her special. Eve didn't have to fight for her special place in Adam's life. When she appeared in the garden and graced life's stage, her importance was established by her presence and existence; nothing else was necessary.

Both men and women need to read Genesis 2 anew and understand what God did. Eve wasn't special because of her size or shape. If women struggle with anything, it is their self-worth and self-esteem. The world constantly tries to build women up, but they miss the real reason they should feel good about themselves. There is nothing physical they need to work on or improve.

Eve wasn't special because she acted "right." The charge often leveled against women is that they have so much attitude. They're accused of being difficult, argumentative, and bossy. These charges are baseless. Yet if one was asked to prove one's worth based on weight, size, looks, or any other thing, anyone might be upset. The Bible's position is—from Eve, to Sarah, to Gomer, to Mary—that every female human being is special, unique, and important because God made her.

She Is Heavenly Presented

The reason men need to read Genesis 2 is to align their minds with the mind of the creator. Every man needs to treat his wife like she is a gift from God. She is his for him, from him, to him. There is no other being like a woman. She is singular, and she is significant. It can't be stressed enough that Eve didn't have to earn her place. Consider the garden scene. How did Adam respond to Eve when he saw her?

His eyes lit up; he saw her and he proclaimed, "This is now!" It's as if he said, "Thank you, God. Now that is what I'm talking about!" Gifts are special for a few reasons. One is because of who gave us the gift; a second is what the gift is and a third reason is the value of the gift. Consider those three as they relate to Eve.

Eve was God-given. Imagine waking up and knowing that God has given you a gift. Genesis 2 records heaven's presentation of woman to the world. Of course men don't own women. And it is precisely this misunderstanding of God's design that men used to mistreat and abuse women. Sadly, it is so far from the beauty of the garden scene and God's intention.

The gift analogy can only be pressed so far; you cannot own human beings. It may be better understood this way. You know the feeling when you receive as a present something that you had never conceptualized could be yours? Or you thought the gift was beyond you? Imagine the experience of being presented this gift.

You look at what is given, and you look at the one who gave it. Your breath is taken away as you say, "This is for me?" The emphasis is on the "me." You can't believe that something so special, so significant, could be yours. Now you realize that it is. That is about as close as I can get to the sense Adam had when Eve walked into the garden. Genesis 2 is Adam and Eve's wedding day.

Maybe we know how Adam felt better than we realize. Remember your wedding day, very likely you had the same experience Adam had. It was when the doors opened, and your wife-to-be stood at the entrance. Everyone stood and turned around—and then she walked in. Your breath was taken away; many a man has cried in that moment. Like Adam, you saw her for the first time. She just walked into the garden of your heart. And you thanked God that she was walking toward you. You could just as well have said, "This is now bone of my bones and flesh of my flesh." In that moment you were Adam. You understand well the concept of "she is for me." You may have even said, "I'm the luckiest man in the world."

Adam had seen the animals; he knew there was nothing there for him. He was put to sleep, and when he woke up, she was there. His breath was taken away, and he essentially exclaimed, "I can't believe she is mine." If you are a husband, you must ask yourself, "How have I treated the gift God gave me?" It is difficult to imagine mistreating God's daughter and heaven's present. Your wife is God's gift to you.

Short of Christ, she is the second-greatest gift heaven has ever given.

She Is Worth the World

Women have intrinsic worth. According to Jesus, her soul is worth more than the rest of creation combined (Matt. 16:26). If a man lost his own soul and gained the whole world what would he give in exchange for his soul? The Lord's point is one soul is worth more than the whole world and if you lose your soul you've lost everything. Nothing physical is worth a soul, not even the whole physical universe. A woman's worth is more than the whole world.

If anyone needs to know this, she does. If you are a woman, you need to know your worth and stop letting outside things determine it for you. She is not her hair, shape, size, shoes, clothes, purses, or makeup. I'm sure that is easy for me to say, seeing I haven't walked a mile in her pumps; for that I apologize, nevertheless it is still true.

Eve never had to tell Adam her worth—he knew it, and she knew it. Eve woke up in the garden and never felt the need to wonder about her place or significance. She was God-made and man's blessing. She is the mother of all living. Only a woman can put that on her resume. Qualifications: "mother of all living." I'd say that is pretty good.

We are as challenged today to convince women of their worth as we are to get men to appreciate it. We are all taught, especially boys early in life, that women are to be exploited. The world teaches us that women are no more than mere objects.

The world teaches us to minimize them and mistreat women. Commercials, movies, games, magazines—every medium today—exploits women. And don't even mention that pornography teaches us that they like it and desire more of it. What a sick misrepresentation of the beauty of the garden. This is having a terrible effect on men, it hurts men's thoughts and actions toward women. Dehumanizing women causes men to think less of women and this harms marriages.

In response to this and other abuses, radical feminists' solution is to turn women into pseudo men. They seek to make women hard, tough, loud, self-promoting divas who declare they don't even need a man. And anything a man can do, a woman can do better, faster, more efficiently, and without blowing stuff up. It turns out this hasn't worked well for us either. There is no battle of the sexes in Genesis 2.

Her beauty, significance, importance, and ability were in her. Adam just recognized it: "She is bone of my bones, flesh of my flesh...she shall be called woman because she was taken out of the man." For this reason, a man gives up every earthly relationship and glues himself to her.

A Plea to Those Who Lead

Men don't own women and never have. Genesis 2 shows the grace of God in giving man what he could not give himself. It shows the glory of woman, the unique creation that, like man, was made in the image of God. It shows the goodness of the home. A man and a woman were married on the first day of human existence. Each was unique and special. God made them capable and able to function in the roles he designed for them.

The entire scene of Genesis 2 is about Adam, but did you notice how much of this chapter was spent talking about Eve. Adam and Eve aren't threatened by each other in the garden. Adam was made first but when he saw Eve he didn't feel the need to tell her that. Instead he focused on the woman God had made for him, and the God who made her.

Equally, Eve didn't have a problem being brought to the man. Notice no words of protest are recorded by Eve. She was from him, for him and brought to him and she is fine with the arrangement. Oh that we could live what God designed. There is no battle of the sexes in Genesis 2. There is only the beauty, glory and honor of the first man and woman who were married on earth, with God as the officiant.

If you are a husband, you must ask yourself, "Do I appreciate heaven's present? Do I recognize her significance, importance, beauty, and ability?" Sadly, the world has convinced men to lower their estimations of women. She is no object; she is not a slave. She is a woman made in the image of God. The singular reason so many women are afraid of and even opposed to male leadership is because men have failed to appreciate and treat accordingly the second greatest gift from God ever given. If you have not treated your wife like a gift from God, what are you willing to do about it?

One more thought to consider, if you are a husband and you have a daughter or even if you don't answer this question. How would you want your daughter's husband to treat her? Well you are married to God's daughter, how are you treating her?

8

CHRIST—THE SECOND ADAM

Reading Genesis 2 is great, and it teaches us how Adam responded to the wonder of Eve when God made her. What it does not tell us is what life was like between the newlyweds on a daily basis. Did Adam continue to dote on Eve? Is this what husbands should infer from the text? Thankfully, we don't have to wonder about Adam's love for Eve because Christ is the second Adam.

What we see in the garden with Adam and Eve is perfected in Christ and his church. Several passages of scripture connect Adam and Christ. Among them are some great lessons on love for their respective brides—Adam and Eve, Christ and the church. One such passage is 1 Corinthians 15:45-49, the text shows the parallels between Adam and Christ. They were both the first men. They were both put to sleep: Adam slept; Christ died. They both stood again, and from their sides, their brides were born. Certainly with Christ and likely with Adam, blood was shed for their brides.

The early portion of this book is committed to explaining *that* men should lead. Christ teaches us *how* men should lead.

Adam Prefigures Christ

> Nevertheless death reigned from Adam to Moses, even
> over them that had not sinned after the similitude of

Adam's transgression, who is the figure of him that was to come. But not as the offence, so also is the free gift. For if through the offence of one many be dead, much more the grace of God, and the gift by grace, which is by one man, Jesus Christ, hath abounded unto many.

And not as it was by one that sinned, so is the gift: for the judgment was by one to condemnation, but the free gift is of many offences unto justification. For if by one man's offence death reigned by one; much more they which receive abundance of grace and of the gift of righteousness shall reign in life by one, Jesus Christ.

Therefore as by the offence of one judgment came upon all men to condemnation; even so by the righteousness of one the free gift came upon all men unto justification of life.

—Romans 5:14–18 (KJV)

In Adam, All Die; in Christ, All Live

But now is Christ risen from the dead, and become the firstfruits of them that slept. For since by man came death, by man came also the resurrection of the dead. For as in Adam all die, even so in Christ shall all be made alive.

—1 Corinthians 15:20–22 (KJV)

For those who lead the home, it is important to remember that God made Eve. Remember that the beauty of the presentation, the gift from God to man, and the glory, splendor, significance, and importance of woman are displayed. Adam's comment about his bride is, "This is now bone of my bones and flesh of my flesh...she shall be called woman because she was taken out of the man." This makes evident his understanding and appreciation of Eve.

In Christ, Love Is Perfected

For Husbands, Christ Is the Example of the Role

Christ is the spiritually perfect Adam. The first Adam was a living soul; the second Adam is a living spirit. Christ also has a bride, and he is pictured with her as Adam was with Eve. In the picture painted for us in the New Testament of the scene in Genesis, Christ takes the place of Adam, and the church takes the place of Eve. The book of Ephesians clearly compares the two.

> And he [God] put all things under his [Christ's] feet and gave him as head over all things to the church, which is his body, the fullness of him who fills all in all.

> —Ephesians 1:22–23

> For the husband is the head of the wife even as Christ is the head of the church, his body, and is himself its Savior.

> —Ephesians 5:23

> Husbands, love your wives, as Christ loved the church and gave himself up for her.

> —Ephesians 5:25

Christ Is the Head of the Church

The first part of Ephesians 5:23 tells us "*the husband is the head of the wife even as Christ is the head of the church.*" This is a deathblow for those who claim there is no role of leadership in marriage. Is Christ over the church? Does Christ lead the church? Does he rule over her? Does the church listen to, follow, and obey Christ? The answer should be yes. Thus, because Christ is over the church, husbands are over their wives.

Christ Is the Savior of the Body
The second half of Ephesians 5:23 tell us that Christ is both the head of and the Savior of his body—his church. Likewise, Eve was from Adam's body (Gen. 2:21–23), and Adam should have been her savior. But he followed her instead of leading her (Gen. 3:17). The Devil deceived Adam's bride and he stood idly by and watched, how tragic.

Christ Loves the Church
Ephesians 5:25 shows how a husband's role in marriage should mirror Christ's role in the church. We don't have to guess about how Adam behaved toward Eve going forward in their life because Christ is the perfection of it. The focus for men should be Christ, the second Adam. The first part of that verse commands, "husbands, love your wives. The word rendered as *love* is the Greek word *agapaō, (a ga pa O)*. Applied to people, it means "to welcome, to entertain, to be fond of, to love dearly" (Thayer, e-sword.com).

Christ Is Our Standard of Love
Ephesians 5:25 also tells us to love "as Christ loved the church and gave himself up for her."

Adam gave up a part of himself for Eve. He was put to sleep and, from his side, a rib was taken. That rib was never given back. But Christ didn't give up just a part of himself for his bride. He gave up his life for her. When reading the New Testament, one should understand that Christ goes to the cross *for his bride*. He is laying down his life for her. He gives up himself for her.

Think about that as you read the passion of the Christ. Hear his agony and see his grief in the garden; look upon his brow as the great drops of sweat as blood fall to the ground. Feel his pain as he turns to his best men during his hour of agony, but they are asleep. Stand next to him as he goes on trial after trial due to his enemies.

Walk out of the garden and meet one of his own who has conspired and betrayed him. Feel the stripes laid upon his back; start with the first and stay until the last as his back is torn apart. See the blood so much that you can no longer tell the source from which it spouts. Listen to the mockery and ridicule and false accusations.

Consider the great contradiction of the perfect Lamb of God being called a liar, insurrectionist, and sinner. Walk with the Christ as he tries desperately to carry his cross but falls under its weight. Stand at the foot of the cross as he is hoisted in the air, suspended between heaven and earth—body mutilated, mind in a daze, feeling neglected, still mocked, still jeered, and finally pierced.

And as you see the blood and water flowing from his side, understand this. He did all of this—he loved in this way; he gave himself up—for her. The New Testament is clear—Christ loves the church, and that love moved Christ to die for her.

How, then should we live?

> Pay careful attention to yourselves and to all the flock, in which the Holy Spirit has made you overseers, to care for the church of God, which he obtained with his own blood.
>
> —Acts 20:28

> By this we know love, that he laid down his life for us, and we ought to lay down our lives for the brothers.
>
> —1 John 3:16

If anyone thinks that a man leading a woman is wrong, see Jesus and the church. If any man thinks that his position gives him some power to abuse his wife, see Jesus. He is to love her as Christ loved the church and gave himself for her. If a man is not willing to do that, he does not deserve a wife.

> The church was for Christ that he might sanctify her, having cleansed her by the washing of water with the word, so that he might present the church to himself in splendor, without spot or wrinkle or any such thing, that she might be holy and without blemish.

> —Ephesians 5:26–27

Eve was from Adam, for Adam, and was brought to Adam in the same way the church is from Christ, for Christ, and these verses indicate that the church is to be brought to Christ that he might wash, cleanse, sanctify, and present her to himself without spot, wrinkle, or blemish.

Putting the three words spot, wrinkle and blemish together here is a paraphrase of what it means. Christ died for the church to place her beside or near him that he might present her as one held in great esteem, honorable and illustrious. She is free from defilement, spot, or even a wrinkle. She is holy, without a blemish, and faultless.

Eve was created in the garden and brought to Adam, and he loved her because of who she was. God made her, and when he finished his creation after Eve, he pronounced everything to be very good, and he stopped working. Christ, the second Adam, died for his bride, and she is the spiritual perfection of Eve.

Husbands Must Imitate Christ

> In the same way husbands should love their wives as their own bodies. He who loves his wife loves himself. For no one ever hated his own flesh, but nourishes and cherishes it, just as Christ does the church.

> —Ephesians 5:28–29

If any husband ever wonders how God expects him to treat his wife, these verses should be read. Love her in the same way as Christ loved the church. Love her for the same reasons Christ loved the church. Love her with the same intentions as Christ loved the church. Love her because of who she is.

The second half of verse 28 adds another layer that removes all doubt and makes clear any confusion. Husbands are to love their wives as their own bodies. There can be no misunderstanding because verse 29 further clarifies it. No man attempting to practice Christianity should ever mistreat or abuse his wife, because no man should abuse himself.

He should rather follow Christ and love his wife to the point of giving his life for her. He should love her as he loves himself. We love ourselves so much that we often struggle with selfishness. In this verse, *nourish* means to "to nourish up to maturity" and *cherish* means "to cherish with tender love, to foster with tender care" (e-sword).

A great picture of this imagery can be seen in the parable that Nathan brought to David after David sinned with Bathsheba. In the parable, Nathan tells David of a rich man who had many flocks and herds and a poor man who had one little ewe lamb. But when a visitor came to see the rich man, instead of taking a lamb from his plenty, he took the poor man's one lamb and killed it for the visitor.

In reading the parable, the love the poor man had for his one little lamb stands out. This is a great picture of nourishing and cherishing:

> There were two men in one city; the one rich, and the other poor. The rich man had exceeding many flocks and herds: But the poor man had nothing, save one little ewe lamb, which he had bought and nourished up: and it grew up together with him, and with his children; it did eat of his own meat, and drank of his own cup, and lay in his bosom, and was unto him as a daughter.
>
> —2 Samuel 12:1–3

If this man could nourish an animal, how much more should a man who pledged his love, life and devotion to his wife nourish and cherish her? The design of God is not the problem; our misunderstanding of it, failure to live it, and desire to change it are the problems. God's instruction for husbands would never lead to abuse; it demands love—a love like Christ's and a love like he loves himself. Another challenge to the relationship is that men often don't love themselves properly.

The things we are taught and believe determine our thoughts and actions. We can't believe men are worthless, good-for-nothing animals and expect them to feel good about ourselves. Tearing down men to build up women ultimately hurts the very women we seek to help. In part because when a man doesn't love himself it makes it difficult if not impossible for him to properly love someone else. It seems especially difficult then to love as Christ loved.

A man should love himself for the same reason a woman should, he is made in the image of God. His soul is worth the whole world. He is not his body, money, career, clothes, status or position. He is a human being who shares the image of God, and if he is a Christian he is God's son. If you love yourself you will be able to properly love your wife.

The Church Is from Christ

For we are members of his body, of his flesh, and of his bones. For this cause shall a man leave his father and mother, and shall be joined unto his wife, and they two shall be one flesh.

- Ephesians 5:28–30

Husbands are instructed to love their wives as Christ loved the church. They are also told to love their wives as they love themselves. These verses add the cause of this love—namely, that the woman is from the man; she is a part of him. The statement about being "members of Christ flesh and bones" harkens back to creation.

When Eve graced the garden, Adam said, "This at last is bone of my bones and flesh of my flesh; she shall be called Woman because she was taken out of Man" (Gen. 2:23). Adam's reaction to Eve is based on his knowledge of her unique nature: "she is like me." But it is more than simply "she is like me"; it is "she is from me." The woman standing before Adam was a part of Adam.

This same idea exists between us and God. God made humans in his image; therefore, we share a likeness to God. God is spirit (John 4:24), and we have an eternal spirit (Gen. 2:7; Zech. 12:1; Heb. 12:9). We not only come from God; we also share the image of God. In a real sense, God loving us is only reasonable because we are like him. To not love us then would be, on some level, to not love himself.

This applied to a man and his wife is the same thing. She is bone of his bones; she is flesh of his flesh. So man ought to love his wife as he loves himself because she came from him. This is the basis for gluing himself to her. The two cannot be separated because they are actually one.

Based on the same reasoning, Paul applies this closeness and oneness to those who are born again into the family of God through Christ because we are members of his body (Eph. 5:30). Just as a man cleaves to his wife above every other earthly relationship, so we should give up all things that seek to come between us and Christ.

A Great Mystery

> This mystery is profound, and I am saying that it refers to Christ and the church. However, let each one of you love his wife as himself, and let the wife see that she respects her husband.
>
> —Ephesians 5:32–33

The great event in Genesis 2 is revealed and expressed in the second Adam and his church. Jesus and his relationship with the church is how men are to love their wives. Eve was the wonder of the garden, the beauty that excelled above all, and the one Adam was to love so deeply he would lay down his life for her. Christ did die for his bride.

There are several important points about Christ and his bride. Christ purposed to be married. Women aren't the only ones who should purpose this great relationship (Eph. 3:9–11). Christ spoke about being married. He was not dragged to the altar; he willingly told others he was going to be married (Matt. 16:18–19). Christ died for his bride. He went beyond theory—he went to the cross and shed his blood for her (Acts 20:28).

Christ is faithful to his bride. Every man should emulate Christ in his marriage. It is one thing to be the head; it is another to be willing to follow your head. Christ is both the head of men and the example of men.

> But I would have you know that the head of every man is Christ, and the head of the woman is the man, and the head of Christ is God.
>
> —1 Corinthians 11:3

Husband, love your wife even as Christ loved the church. God designed you to lead her, Christ showed you how to love her.

9

GOD'S WORD TO THOSE WHO LEAD

The challenges and difficulties of marriage make it easy to get away from God's design. When this happens, more problems ensue. What we must do is remember that each of us is connected to and responsible to God. The Word of God must be able to instruct, warn, direct, and guide us. If I am unwilling to listen to God's Word, I will be unwilling to listen to God's Word in my marriage. Whether I am leading or following, I must do so by God's Word.

God designed marriage, and he expects us to follow him. Having created us in his image, God expects that we will think and behave as he does. This is reasonable since he is the father of spirits (Heb. 12:9), and we are his offspring (Acts 17:28). The practice of Christianity must be applied to your marriage, not simply lived out in the world. Let your light so shine begins at home. Jesus, the apostles, and the prophets also taught us some specific ways in which we are to behave like God.

God's Expectations of Us

Love Like He Does

> You have heard that it was said, "You shall love your neighbor and hate your enemy." But I say to you, Love your enemies and pray for those who persecute you, so

that you may be sons of your Father who is in heaven. For he makes his sun rise on the evil and on the good, and sends rain on the just and on the unjust. For if you love those who love you, what reward do you have? Do not even the tax collectors do the same? And if you greet only your brothers, what more are you doing than others? Do not even the Gentiles do the same? You therefore must be perfect, as your heavenly Father is perfect.

—Matthew 5:43–48

Show Mercy Like He Does

But love your enemies, and do good, and lend, expecting nothing in return, and your reward will be great, and you will be sons of the Most High, for he is kind to the ungrateful and the evil. Be merciful, even as your Father is merciful.

—Luke 6:35–36

Forgive Like He Does

Let all bitterness and wrath and anger and clamor and slander be put away from you, along with all malice. Be kind to one another, tenderhearted, forgiving one another, as God in Christ forgave you.

—Ephesians 4:31–32

Endure Suffering Like He Does

For to this you have been called, because Christ also suffered for you, leaving you an example, so that you might follow in his steps. He committed no sin, neither was deceit found in his mouth. When he was reviled, he did not revile in return; when he suffered, he did not threaten, but continued entrusting himself to him who judges justly.

—1 Peter 2:21–23

Being God's leader demands that we first follow God. The head of every man is Christ (1 Cor. 11:3). Don't forgive, show mercy and suffer for everyone in the world and then act rude, unmerciful and unloving toward your wife. As a husband you must ask yourself, am I behaving like God?

God's Expectations of Leaders
When it comes to leadership, God's expectations continue because those who lead represent him. Therefore, he always has clear instructions for and expectations of them. God's expectations rest on individual responsibility and personal accountability.

God's actions toward the first man and the first sin are powerful in what they teach of God's expectations of those who lead. God commanded Adam about which trees he couldn't eat of in the garden:

But of the tree of the knowledge of good and evil you shall not eat, for in the day that you eat of it you shall surely die.

—Genesis 2:17

Genesis 3 records the first sin of mankind against God. Eve ate the fruit of the tree and gave it to her husband, who was with her, and he did eat. After eating, their eyes were opened, they made coverings for themselves, and they hid. God approached them and called out to Adam.

As a leader it is imperative that you learn the lessons from this conversation.

God and Adam (Gen. 3:9–12)

> But the LORD God called to the man and said to him, "Where are you?" And he said, "I heard the sound of you in the garden, and I was afraid, because I was naked, and I hid myself." He said, "Who told you that you were naked? Have you eaten of the tree of which I commanded you not to eat?" The man said, "The woman whom you gave to be with me, she gave me fruit of the tree, and I ate."
>
> —Genesis 3:9–12

There are a series of questions in this passage:

1. Where are you?
2. Who told you that you were naked?
3. Did you eat of the tree I commanded you not to eat?

Adam responds to each of God's questions, and God holds him accountable for his answers. What can we learn from this interchange?

1. We are individually responsible for being faithful to God.
2. We will be held individually accountable for our faithfulness to God.
3. Our personal actions are the basis for judgment, which leads to reward or punishment.

The basis of expectation is God's Word. After speaking to Eve and the serpent, God spoke again to Adam. Closely consider his words:

> And to Adam he said, "Because you have listened to the voice of your wife and have eaten of the tree of which I commanded you, 'You shall not eat of it,' cursed is the

ground because of you; in pain you shall eat of it all
the days of your life."

—Genesis 3:17

God told Adam which trees were allowed and which one was forbidden.
God expected Adam to follow his command. Adam did not listen to
God; he listened to the voice of his wife. She gave him the fruit, and he
ate it. Eve argued that the serpent had deceived her, so she ate the fruit.
God's expectation was that each person would be obedient to his Word.

When God approached, questioned, and punished Adam and Eve,
it was his Word that was used as the basis for their judgment. It is also
his Word that will be the basis for our judgment. Consider these verses:

For we must all appear before the judgment seat of
Christ, so that each one may receive what is due for
what he has done in the body, whether good or evil.

—2 Corinthians 5:10

This is so important because those who lead must know what God
has said to them about what he expects of them. Regardless whether
one does or does not lead according to God's Word, God will one day
judge him by that standard. No one will be able to offer God excuses
about his disobedience, neglect, or abuse of position.

Adam should teach us that God will not accept excuses for our
disobedience. Adam said it was Eve's fault, Eve said it was the serpent's fault, but everyone was punished individually and held personally responsible for their actions. When God asks you questions about
your behavior in your marriage what will you say? The world told me
not to lead, the world said male leadership was mean, rude, old and
outdated. My preacher told me it was born out of cultural ignorance
and Paul was just expressing his opinion. My wife wanted to lead and

I didn't see anything wrong with letting her. I was afraid and so I did nothing. If God's question is, did you lead like I designed, did you love like Christ exemplified, what will you say?

So that we don't offer God excuses, it would be helpful, then, to know what God has said to those who lead.

First let's consider some biblical examples of the kind of men and the kind of character God demanded of those who led his people, then let's apply those principals to husbands (emphasis in verses added ELO).

Rulers in Israel—Jethro's Instruction to Moses

And Moses' father in law said unto him, The thing that thou doest is not good. Thou wilt surely wear away, both thou, and this people that is with thee: for this thing is too heavy for thee; thou art not able to perform it thyself alone. Hearken now unto my voice, I will give thee counsel, and God shall be with thee: Be thou for the people to God-ward, that thou mayest bring the causes unto God: And thou shalt teach them ordinances and laws, and shalt shew them the way wherein they must walk, and the work that they must do. Moreover thou shalt provide out of all the people able men, *such as fear God, men of truth, hating covetousness;* and place such over them, to be rulers of thousands, and rulers of hundreds, rulers of fifties, and rulers of tens.

—Exodus 18:17–22 KJV

Elders

This is a true saying, If a man desire the office of a bishop, he desireth a good work. A bishop then must be *blameless, the husband of one wife, vigilant, sober, of good behaviour, given to hospitality, apt to teach; Not given to wine, no striker, not greedy of filthy lucre; but patient, not a brawler, not covetous*; One that ruleth well his own house, having his children in subjection with all gravity; (For if a man know not how to rule his own house, how shall he take care of the church of God?) Not a novice, lest being lifted up with pride he fall into the condemnation of the devil. Moreover he must have a good report of them which are without; lest he fall into reproach and the snare of the devil.

—1 Timothy 3:1–7 KJV

This is why I left you in Crete, so that you might put what remained into order, and appoint elders in every town as I directed you—if anyone is above reproach, the husband of one wife, and his children are believers and not open to the charge of debauchery or insubordination. For an overseer, as God's steward, must be above reproach. He must *not be arrogant or quick-tempered or a drunkard or violent or greedy for gain, but hospitable, a lover of good, self-controlled, upright, holy, and disciplined. He must hold firm to the trustworthy word* as taught, so that he may be able to give instruction in sound doctrine and also to rebuke those who contradict it.

—Titus 1:5–9 KJV

So I exhort the elders among you, as a fellow elder and a witness of the sufferings of Christ, as well as a partaker in the glory that is going to be revealed:

shepherd the flock of God that is among you, *exercising oversight, not under compulsion, but willingly, as God would have you; not for shameful gain, but eagerly; not domineering over those in your charge, but being examples* to the flock.

—1 Peter 5:1–3 KJV

Deacons

Deacons likewise must be d*ignified, not double-tongued, not addicted to much wine, not greedy for dishonest gain. They must hold the mystery of the faith with a clear conscience.* And let them also be tested first; then let them serve as deacons if they prove themselves blameless. Their wives likewise must be dignified, not slanderers, but soberminded, faithful in all things. Let deacons each be the husband of one wife, managing their children and their own households well.

—1 Timothy 3:8–12

Parents

Fathers, do not provoke your children to anger, but bring them up in the discipline and instruction of the Lord.

—Ephesians 6:4

Fathers, do not provoke your children, lest they become discouraged.

—Colossians 3:21

Masters of Servants (Bosses/Employees)

Masters, do the same to them, and stop your threatening, knowing that he who is both their Master and yours is in heaven, and that there is no partiality with him.

—Ephesians 6:9

Husbands

Husbands, *love your wives, even as Christ also loved the church,* and gave himself for it...So ought men to love their wives as their own bodies. He that loveth his wife loveth himself. For no man ever yet hated his own flesh; but nourisheth and cherisheth it, even as the Lord the church... For this cause shall a man leave his father and mother, and shall be joined unto his wife, and they two shall be one flesh...*Nevertheless let every one of you in particular so love his wife even as himself.*

—Ephesians 5:25–33 KJV

The husband should give to his wife her conjugal rights... Likewise the husband does not have authority over his own body, but the wife does...*Do not deprive one another,* except perhaps by agreement for a limited time, that you may devote yourselves to prayer; but then come together again, so that Satan may not tempt you because of your lack of self-control.

—1 Corinthians 7:3–5

Husbands, love your wives, and do not be harsh with them. (ESV)

Husbands, love your wives, and be not bitter against them. (KJV)

—Colossians 3:19

Likewise, husbands, *live with your wives in an understanding way, showing honor to the woman* as the weaker vessel, since they are heirs with you of the grace of life, so that your prayers may not be hindered.

—1 Peter 3:7 KJV

God's Expectations Applied Putting The Pieces Together

God Expects Godly Leaders

Moses chose able men who feared God; Paul wrote that leaders were to be godly. The leader is to have a pious disposition and a committed heart that is exclusive to Jehovah. He is to know and be moved by the fear of the Lord. That reverent disposition will serve him well as he holds the mystery of the faith in a good or clear conscience.

Leaders should know who they represent and allow that knowledge to inform and temper their actions. The fear of the Lord is the beginning of wisdom (Prov. 1:7). Those who lead for God should be in awe of God. Every leader must know that this is God's expectation. He will be held responsible for how he behaves toward God.

God Expects Spiritual Leaders

The leader is to know who he represents, and he is to know what the one he represents has said. Moses was told to pick men of truth.

One of the first temptations of leading is to be dishonest. It is easy to change the standards that one applies to oneself and to others. Men of truth should have their thoughts and actions guarded and guided by the God of truth and the Word of truth. The spiritual leader reads God's Word, he devotes himself to prayer, and he lives the Word of God. He loves as Christ loves because God's spiritual word directs his spiritual life. Did you know that the kings of Israel were commanded to write their own copy of the law and read then live and govern by it (Deut. 17:14-20).

God Expects Faithful Leaders

God doesn't ask you to be sinless, but he demands that you are faithful. Consider again the language of scripture to describe leaders. A bishop then must be blameless, above reproach, not open to the charge of debauchery or insubordination (Titus 1:6). Faithfulness is not flawlessness but it is one who trusts in the Lord with all his heart (Proverbs 3:5). His trust in God, fueled by his spiritual mind-set, directs his steps and those he leads toward God.

God Expects Reasonable Leaders

There is little in the world more frustrating and difficult to deal with than an unreasonable leader. The God of heaven, who is perfect in every way, has on numerous occasions listened to men and reasoned with them. Abraham had questions of God, maybe even misunderstandings of God, and was given an audience with God. God reasoned with Abraham about the destruction of Sodom and Gomorrah and moved at his request (Gen. 18:23–33).

God's people became so sinful he no longer wanted them to even bring sacrifices. In this sinful rebellious state, he offered them an opportunity to come and reason with him. He promised if they repented, he would cleanse them:

> Wash yourselves; make yourselves clean; remove the
> evil of your deeds from before my eyes; cease to do

evil, learn to do good; seek justice, correct oppression; bring justice to the fatherless, plead the widow's cause. "Come now, let us reason together, says the LORD: though your sins are like scarlet, they shall be as white as snow; though they are red like crimson, they shall become like wool. If you are willing and obedient, you shall eat the good of the land; but if you refuse and rebel, you shall be eaten by the sword; for the mouth of the LORD has spoken."

—Isaiah 1:16–20

Men are to learn from God and imitate him for those they lead. You are to be sound of mind, self-controlled, and even-tempered; you are to curb your desires and impulses. Being a leader should not a dictator make. Elders are forbidden from lording over God's heritage; fathers are told not to provoke their children to wrath. Leaders can and should be questioned; that is not to be confused with being challenged. An unreasonable leader is nothing like the God of heaven.

God Expects Righteous Leaders

The words used to describe those who lead in the varied positions make a strong statement about their characters. They must be ones who do right. They are fair, balanced, and impartial. Their judgments are even-handed. They would never receive a bribe or pervert justice because of whom this decision would impact.

This list of expressions screams that this is to be a man who treats his fellow man righteously, how much more his wife.

Be not bitter.
Be above reproach.
Be thou an example.
Do not be harsh.

Not quick tempered.
Dwell in an understanding way.

God is just and fair in all of his dealings. No one will ever accurately accuse God of injustice or unrighteousness. God's scales of justice are balanced; he often gives man mercy and tempers the punishment he is due. The eighteenth chapter of Ezekiel is dedicated to demonstrating God's fairness in dealing with his people:

> The soul who sins shall die. The son shall not suffer for the iniquity of the father, nor the father suffer for the iniquity of the son. The righteousness of the righteous shall be upon himself, and the wickedness of the wicked shall be upon himself.
>
> —Ezekiel 18:20

> Have I any pleasure in the death of the wicked, declares the Lord GOD, and not rather that he should turn from his way and live? But when a righteous person turns away from his righteousness and does injustice and does the same abominations that the wicked person does, shall he live? None of the righteous deeds that he has done shall be remembered; for the treachery of which he is guilty and the sin he has committed, for them he shall die. Yet you say, "The way of the Lord is not just." Hear now, O house of Israel: Is my way not just? Is it not your ways that are not just?"
>
> —Ezekiel 18:23–25

God's ways are just are yours? Men who represent God must have the qualities of fairness and even-handedness if they will please God. Are you fair to your wife?

God Expects Leaders Who Love His People

Leaders of God's people are to have the heart of God toward his people. John tells us that God is love (1 John 4:8). To lead is to love; leaders are to be hospitable and lovers of good men. That love is to regard the person for who he or she is, not what he or she can offer. God loved us when we were sinners and sent his Son to die for our sins (Rom. 5:6–8).

You must emulate God's love toward those he leads and live as an example of those you lead. A house divided against itself cannot stand. And where there is a lack of love, there will be strife, envy, and every evil work. The church at Corinth lacked love, and the result is nearly a problem in every chapter. The more excellent way is love (1 Cor. 13), and love is certainly the way of the Lord.

When God's people are loved by his leaders, they will be cared for, watched after, and regarded the way God does. This will certainly please him. God's expectations of those who lead is real, and he will hold them accountable. Leaders represent God, and he expects them to behave like he does.

God's Expectation of Husbands Can You Say These Things

Godly men – I will walk in the fear of the Lord.

Spiritual men – God's word will develop my character and govern my life.

Faithful men – I will be committed to God exclusively.

Righteous men – I will be fair and just in my dealings with my wife.

Reasonable men – I will be an approachable balanced man with my wife.

Sober-minded men – I will be of a sound mind and considerate of my wife.

If I am a leader, I must lead like God, and I must remember that God will hold me personally accountable for obeying his Word. Husband you must know and live God's expectations of you.

10

MY WIFE WON'T REVERENCE
ME—WHAT CAN I DO?

Both men and women have shown themselves very capable of disobeying God. Adam and Eve sinned in the garden. Marriage is no different. Men do wrong; women do wrong—not in any particular order. The one wronged usually scales the tower of victimhood, reaches the roof of self-righteousness. From this perch they then execute as much wrong as he or she has received but pardons the crimes because they were justified to do wrong, because they wronged first.

There are individuals who believe that a wife has a right to refuse to reverence her husband if the reason is good enough. This is not true, but some people seem to think so. This chapter is intended for the man who is trying to be the spiritual leader of his home but has or is contemplating giving up God's charge because of his wife's actions.

Therefore, before we suggest things you can do, let us consider some reasons your wife might be refusing to reverence you. Next we will notice some things you can't do if she won't reverence you. Finally, we will move on to things you can do if your wife won't reverence you.

She May Disagree with Your Right to Lead

If she practices radical feminism, she will disagree with the design of male leadership. This will be sufficient for her not to follow you. In so doing, she believes you are equal in roles and that leadership is shared. Therefore, she never sees herself as "following" you; she sees you as co-leaders at best. Often this dynamic ends with her leading, because there is no such thing as a leaderless home. Her voice will be the one heard most and followed most frequently.

She May Be Misinformed

Not everyone who ends up in the previous place does so with evil intention. She may have come from a background where women led their husbands. Female leadership may be all she has ever known, and maybe you have contributed to the problem. When you were dating, if you shared everything and if you often defaulted to her, she might be confused when this dynamic changes in marriage. It's likely that she thought when you were married, this sharing of responsibility would continue. She never took over because you always shared the lead; thus, she may be ignorant of male leadership.

You Asked Her to Lead

She is not following, but it is not because she refuses to follow; rather, it's because you asked her to lead. Some men have attempted to gift the authority God has given them to their wives. These men have disobeyed God and done their wives a great disservice. No man has the right or power to take what God has designed and change it to fit his desires.

No human can give someone power or the right to disobey God. Aaron the priest couldn't take the leadership of the priesthood from Levi and give it to another tribe? Not even Jesus could be a priest under the Law of Moses because our Lord was from the tribe of Judah (Heb. 7:12–15). Any husband who has given his wife the right to lead him and their family should go to her and ask for it back.

You Are Not Doing What You Need To Do

This may be the most popular reason that wives give for refusing to follow their husbands and reverence them. If this is the reason given, it was likely not reached lightly. Those who do this find themselves in an impossible situation in their minds. They know that what they are about to do is contrary to their vow and God's design, and yet they feel compelled to do it anyway. Some possible reasons follow.

Financial Mismanagement

Some men have wasted more money than BP wasted oil in the gulf. Wives have pled and pled for them not to mismanage their money, but their husbands did things their way. Perhaps a wife has prayed to God for her man to change, but he hasn't. In private and to close friends, she has cried a river of tears but went down the river with no paddle. She knew her family would be ruined financially, and she has watched it happen. They have suffered loss of goods, name, and reputation. If these things are true of her, she felt that she had to do something, so she stopped following and reverencing him so she is now trying to handle things herself.

Immoral Sexual Behavior

This could range from adultery to other forms of fornication. Some husbands have cheated on their wives. She suspected it, confronted him, and it was finally confirmed. There are women who have endured this multiple times and have stayed, forgiven, and tried to make it work. The wife has endured lies, shame, hurt, betrayal, and the total loss of trust. This is so damaging to a relationship that it is the one reason God allows for divorce.

Other men have given themselves to pornography. The wife has caught him, confronted him, and it still continues. She's cried, shouted, and threatened, but he has only sought to become more skilled at hiding it. A husband's use of pornography does a terrible disservice to his wife. Using pornorgraphy harms her self-esteem, hurts the relationship, and destroys her trust in him, it also hurts the user.

If neither of these is the problem, it might be that he is a chronic flirt or that he constantly looks at other women. He has never met a stranger, and his excuse to his wife is that women are just being friendly. It is exceedingly disrespectful to one's wife to flirt with, touch, or constantly stare at other women. This can even happen at church—his wife sees the way he looks at all of the sisters and hears how he compliments them. Through it all, she stands there and puts on a happy face. All the while her reverence for him has slowly dissipated into nothingness.

Poor Leadership Skills

He does not manage himself or any aspect of his life well. He mismanages his time; he does not keep his word. He starts things and stops them almost as quickly. There is nothing solid and reliable about his life, and she can't follow that. She is more of the rock of the family than he has ever been. He has great plans that never come to fruition; conversely, she plans better, knows better, and feels certain she has to do something.

These could be some of the reasons she has concluded that he is not doing what he is supposed to do. Of course, any husband reading this may have an opposing view of everything said. He might dispute why she isn't following, but the point is that she isn't. He is not being reverenced, and he knows that he should be. Since his wife will not, what can he do about it? Before we address what we he can do, let's notice some things he can't do with God's approval.

What a Husband Cannot Do

You Cannot Turn Over the Reins of Leadership

If you're guilty of the things mentioned above, you need to repent and get right with God. Your failures are first against God and then against your wife. David told us all that when we sin, it is against God: "Against thee and thee only have I sinned" (Psalm 51:4). You might be tempted to give up and stop leading out of a sense of guilt for your wrongs because she deserves better.

Of course, she deserves better, but giving her better does not mean giving her leadership. You cannot give up leadership in order to gain peace. Her issue is not your leadership; it is your sin. The way to peace is to give up sin in your life. The solution to sin is repentance, not concession. The role is established by God, and we will never improve our lives by disobeying him.

You Cannot Be Harsh or Bitter

Because you might dispute the claims for why she isn't following, some men might be tempted to become harsh or bitter toward their wives. God will not endorse this action, for he has already commanded, "Husbands love your wives, and be not harsh (bitter) toward them" (Col. 3:19). Harsh speech, rough treatment, and mean words will not encourage any wife to follow her husband. Certainly, God will not approve of such actions.

You Cannot Return Evil for Evil

Maybe the shortest distance to travel in the world is the space between being done wrong and starting to do wrong. This is especially true if you see her failure to follow as rebellion or an act of aggression. It is amazing how tempting it is to harm the one who harms you. While it might be tempting, it is not right. God clearly instructs that we are not to return evil for evil (Rom. 12:17). If a man feels he is not being followed and he is doing what is right, he must not begin to do wrong in return. If doing right will not cause his wife to follow him, how can he think doing wrong to her will?

You Cannot Retreat and Go AWOL

Every man who gives up and quits on his wife and family is absent without leave. We all agreed with God and gave our word to him that marriage is until death do us part. Our commitment is for better or worse, for richer or poorer, in sickness and in health; we promised we would forsake all others as long as we both shall live. We said it, God heard it, and witnesses saw it. And if that weren't enough, we sealed it with the rings on our fingers. Now we are engaged in the war, and the battle has been joined. A great many things happen on the battlefield. There are victories and defeats; there are strategic retreats and evasive maneuvers. But retreating to fight no more is surrender; retreating to leave the battlefield is desertion. You can adapt and overcome, but you cannot quit on your marriage.

You Cannot Turn Away from God

The first casualty of war is truth. God is the truth, and unfortunately God often becomes the first casualty of war when husbands and wives are fighting. We often make the triangle of man, woman, and God. But we fail to recognize that when the man and woman break their covenant with each other, they also break it with God. The triangle is the best angle because it is the "try" angle. Consider a triangle with God at the top, the husband at one side and the wife at the other. The husband and wife are the furthest apart at the bottom; as they move toward the top of the triangle, they get closer to each other. It is so important to remember that when we get closer to God, we get closer to each other. How you and God are doing in your relationship is a great indicator of how you and your wife are doing.

No matter what you decide to do you can't do any of the aforementioned with God's approval. If this is your life situation now is the time to draw closer to God. Trying to build your house while rejecting the Divine architect's blueprint is building on sinking sand and will inevitably end in failure.

What Can a Husband Do?

You Can Pray to God

This is why you must remain faithful to God because he who refuses to hear God's law, even his prayers are an abomination to God (Prov.

28:9). And Peter said that husbands who don't treat their wives as God desires their prayers will be hindered (1 Pet. 3:7).

If your wife will not follow or reverence you, you should spend a lot of time in prayer. You should pray for yourself. These prayers are for your heart that you will not become bitter and return evil for evil. Pray for strength to follow the example of Jesus, who, when he was threatened, didn't threaten back but committed himself to God (1 Pet. 2:21–25).

After praying for yourself, pray for your wife. Christ taught us to pray for those who despitefully use us and persecute us. While she may see it differently, if you believe her to be adversarial, pray for her. The fact that she is not following does not determine your actions; she is your wife, and you should pray for her. A righteous man's prayers avail much (James 5:16). Anyone who is not living as God desires is in need of prayer; how much more are those we love and have pledged our lives to?

Also, spend a lot of time in conversation with God about your children and his family's futures. There are always casualties of war and collateral damage. Children suffer when mom and dad are at war. The damage done is often not considered as dad's and mom's fight for their positions. You should not stay for the children; this is the wrong outlook. To think in terms of staying doesn't address the problem.

Instead, through God's Word, you should, seek resolution to the problem and remain in a happy, godly marriage. It is reasonable to consider what effects divorce will have on one's children. One need also consider what staying and mistreating each other will do. The solution is not to leave or stay; it is to change and improve spiritually.

Everybody claims to believe in prayer when they don't need to pray. But when things get rough and times get hard, people stop praying to God and start taking matters into their own hands. Prayer was never designed to be a get-out-of-jail-free card; play Monopoly for one of those. Prayer is designed to provide comfort, strength, and motivation to continue fighting the good fight of faith. You must fight but are you fighting the right battle. Are you fighting the good fight of faith have you laid hold of eternal life (1 Tim. 6:12).

Paul gave us a great description of prayer and its power:

> Let your reasonableness be known to everyone. The Lord is at hand; do not be anxious about anything, but in everything by prayer and supplication with thanksgiving let your requests be made known to God. And the peace of God, which surpasses all understanding, will guard your hearts and your minds in Christ Jesus. Finally, brothers, whatever is true, whatever is honorable, whatever is just, whatever is pure, whatever is lovely, whatever is commendable, if there is any excellence, if there is anything worthy of praise, think about these things. What you have learned and received and heard and seen in me—practice these things, and the God of peace will be with you.
>
> —Philippians 4:5–9

In prayer, the peace of God is beyond understanding. In Christ, our hearts and minds are guarded. This is greatly aided when we think of the things that are good, honorable, true, just, and lovely. The Bible also tells us to refuse to be anxious about anything. Prayer is not gender specific. All Christians need to pray and when the need is greatest the prayer needs to match the need. Christ spoke of a woman praying until an unjust judge finally gave her, her request. The point the Lord was making by the purpose of the parable is this. And he told them a parable to the effect that they ought always to pray and not lose heart (Luke 18:1).

Perhaps your wife is refusing to follow and reverence you. Perhaps she has led the family and you have pled, argued, and fought for the right to lead, but the family is now a mess. Perhaps time has gone by, lives have been affected, and years and decades have been lost. You have become harsh, distant, and cold, and you are ready to give up and leave.

What should you do? You should pray as hard and as faithfully as you ever have. Pray for your thoughts and actions toward your wife; pray for her, and pray for the children. We can lose battles, but we cannot lose our families. When the people of Israel wanted to kill Moses, he prayed for them (Num. 14:1–20). When Jesus was on the cross he prayed for those who put him there. When Stephen was being stoned he prayed for those who threw the stones. God will approve of us praying for our wives; he will not approve of us quitting on our wives and marriage.

Husband, ask yourself, "When I feel my wife is doing the most wrong, what do I do?" If the answer is not "pray for myself, for her, and for our family" then start praying now more than you ever have. Prayer doesn't require God to change our circumstances; prayer asks God to change us within them. Jesus prayed in the garden and then went to the cross. Will you pray and then obey?

You Can Examine Yourself

Have you examined yourself in the mirror of God's word or do you just continue to insist you're right? Leadership begins with the leader; it always has, and it always will. If a team has quit on its coach, is it reasonable to take a look at the coach? What if a congregation is not following the pastors or a company its management? If these things are true, one should apply the same thinking to a husband and wife.

If your family is not what it ought to be, do not assume the followers are the problem; certainly they can be, but first examine the leader. Every husband must examine himself in light of God's Word. The Word of God is likened to a mirror, and leaders need to look into it to see if they are what God desires. This is a self-examination; not an interrogation for no one likes to be examined by others without requesting it.

A husband need not seek perfection in himself, but he should be open-minded and honest enough to admit his mistakes and change if necessary. He examines himself, and in doing so, he must ask himself, "Did I do what God told me to do?" The examination is not necessarily to approve or disprove any accusation. He is not trying to prove where he is right and she is wrong. He is measuring himself against the standard of God and the example of Christ.

Not only is examination a command (2 Cor. 13:5); it is also beneficial. When we examine ourselves, we can see the spots and wrinkles on our clothes and faces. Seeing God and ourselves will temper our actions and reactions toward others. God has expectations of those who lead, and they need to be God's men. This is not always synonymous with agreeing with your wife, though it may be in some instances.

By examining yourself, you might realize the need to repent for sins against God. If you sinned against your wife you owe her an apology. Remember that Peter said she is your sister and heir together of the grace of life (1 Pet. 3:7). You cannot control your wife, but you can examine yourself

You Can Search the Scriptures
The right of a husband to lead his wife comes from God. In reading the scriptures, you will be reminded of this fact and be strengthened to live it. You have the right to make decisions for your family and to determine which direction you go. Not only do you have the right you also have the responsibility. Should your family end in ruin, God will hold you accountable. Call a family meeting and reaffirm this God given right. You don't need to yell, scream, or beat your chest; instead, he needs to reason, plead, and explain using God's Word.

He needs confidence that it is God's design and that he is able and capable. His right to be followed resides in scripture. He should lead his family by following God. This would be a great time to seek God's wisdom and apply it to his life and leadership (Prov. 2:6). In reading scripture, he will read how God dealt with his people when they didn't follow him. The book of Judges shares God's long-suffering and mercy.

Reading the life of Christ and following his example will aid him as he considers his family. Jesus was perfect, and people did him wrong, questioned him, and even lied about him. His friends betrayed, denied, and abandoned him. If a husband has ever felt similarly treated, Jesus is the example to emulate. When trouble comes, the mind of Christ will enable him to walk in the steps of the Savior (Phil. 2:5; 1 Pet. 2:21–25).

You Can Seek Counsel

Everyone who leads has recourse when followers don't follow. Moses appealed to God when Israel refused to follow. The government can imprison, punish, and even execute citizens who are unruly. Elders can call the congregation together and withdraw fellowship from members who walk disorderly and refuse to repent. When husbands have wives who refuse to submit, reverence, and follow them, there are things he can do.

We have mentioned prayer, self-examination, and reading the scriptures. You can also schedule an appointment with the elders and ask for counsel and guidance. Spiritual leaders can sit with the couple and hear both sides. Both can share and have their say with a neutral, impartial, spiritual third party. If everyone desires to please God, such a meeting should surely help relieve the situation. Some frown on spiritual leaders because often they are not professional marriage counselors. This should not prevent help being provided, but if some should seek further help, then they should suggest seeing a professional marriage counselor, who counsels in harmony with God's word.

You Can Talk With Your Wife

Talking with her is not the same as talking to her or at her. Inform her of your concerns and ask for and listen to her side of the situation. There are several sides to every relationship. Don't be dismissive of her concerns, yet this is not a negotiation; it is an intervention. The iceberg is ahead the cliff is approaching if we continue on this track, we are sure to sink or fall over the edge. You are not seeking her approval; you are seeking her acceptance of God's design. In order to convey your feelings clearly, use illustrations or draw word pictures. Share how her refusal to follow makes you feel. You might even write a letter; writing a letter can allow us to share our thoughts without being interrupted. Writing can also prevent conversations from escalating into arguments.

You Must Continue To Love Your Wife

Three times in Ephesian 5, God tells a husband to love his wife. If God says something once, it is sufficient. Husbands we must pay attention when God says the same thing multiple times within a few verses: "Husbands, love your wives, even as Christ also loved the church, and gave himself for it" (Eph. 5:25); "So ought men to love their wives as their own bodies. He that loveth his wife loveth himself" (5:28); "Nevertheless let every one of you in particular so love his wife even as himself; and the wife see that she reverence her husband" (5:33).

Loving your wife does not always mean agreeing with her; neither does it mean always approving of her actions. We should not think this strange, because God continues to love us though he does not always agree with or approve of our actions. God has commanded every husband to love his wife. When men get married they vow before God and witnesses to do so. His love for her is never dependent upon her actions. She does not have to earn his love, and he must and not withhold it from her. Jesus used the same word when he told us to love our enemies (Matt. 5:43–45).

Don't Confuse Love with Like

Jesus never told us to like our enemies, because that is impossible. No one will like being mistreated, but if our enemies are in need of help, their humanity demands that we help them. The man who happens upon his enemy half dead in the street owes it to the man to help him. He doesn't have to like him; he needs to love him.

When we are dating, we put our best foot forward and behave the best we can to please the other person. The result of this interaction is that we like being around each other. We enjoy each other's company, and when we are apart, we long to get back together. During this time, we like to hear each other's ideas and thoughts. We like learning about each other; we like giving and sharing with each other. She can do very little wrong in our eyes; we just like her so much. We use the word *love*, but it is more accurately "like." In fact, we like each other so much that we decide that we want to spend the rest of our lives together.

So we get married, and for whatever reason, our best behavior reverts to normal behavior. Our words cease to be as nice and sweet as they once were, and we hurt each other. The words, ideas, and feelings we once liked hearing become sources of pain and discomfort. Her ideas and thoughts are now nagging and noise that you wish would stop. Of course, we begin to blame each other for the problem and convince ourselves that we are "falling out of love."

We probably never understood love as Christ lived it and commanded it. What is more likely true is that we have been "falling out of *like*." Maybe now would be a good time to learn the love of God as exemplified by Christ on the cross: "By this we know love, that he laid down his life for us, and we ought to lay down our lives for the brothers" (1 John 3:16). When we do we can live like Christ did toward his enemies (Rom. 5:6–8). Surely, none of us can believe Christ liked being in the garden and going to the cross.

Scripture tells husbands to love their wives, even if those wives do not follow them or are disagreeable or even if they have "reasons" for not following and feel they are justified because of a husband's failings. God still loved us. Jesus still loved us while we were at our worst, and Christ died for us. No man following God is free to cast aside God's Word because he is hurt.

Chances are really good that what you are experiencing is that you don't like your wife, or at least her actions. But ask yourself this: why did you like her in the first place? Like is reciprocal; while you were dating, you both invested in the like bank, have you stopped? In marriage, life happens, and several things have happened: we've changed, we hurt each other, and we disagree with each other.

We have yelled at, manipulated, and lied to each other. We have failed to be what each of us thought we were getting. We have aged, and we have told each other in word and deed that we are no longer worth the effort. Not amazingly, we don't like this kind of relationship, and it bears no resemblance to when we were dating. If you want to change it begin a reinvestment plan in your wife.

You Can Have Hope

You can love your wife because God and Christ loves you. By humbling yourself before God, appreciating his mercy, and learning his love, we can change ourselves. We are fighting, feuding, and arguing because of our pride. We can't believe someone could do us this wrong—while all along, we wrong God. Learning from God can change us; then we can seek each other's highest good. Come to grips with the fact that your situation is the reality you have built then strive to construct a new reality. We must get over ourselves and come down from our perches of self-righteousness and instead ask God for help (Luke 18:9–14).

We can agree to behave outside of our situation and love each other. By doing this, we can draw a line in the sand and refuse to go backward. It will help us both if we stop crying over the past and wishing it were different. There is a reason it is the past, so let's vow to leave it there. We can make a new reality and leave anger and resentment behind.

There is hope for our marriages as long as we hope in God. One way to help is to look forward. Approximate the years you have left on earth and decide how you want to live them together. Do you want to live with God or without God, do you want to be married or divorced, in misery or happiness. I'd rather live together happily and healthily than miserably and sadly. The Lord left us an example, and he assures us that we can be like him. Christ loved his enemies and died for us (Rom. 5:6–8). When followers won't follow, leaders must continue to lead us to God.

Friend you have to know, that if you do what this chapter says you must not do while refusing to do what the chapter says you must do your actions will harm your marriage not your wife's actions. You will hurt your own life because hate, rage and vengeance will destroy you from the inside out. You will harm your wife's life because she will be the recipient of your bad actions. You will hurt your children's lives because they will learn from you and follow your example.

No husband can control his wife, and God has never charged any husband to submit his wife. She is charged with doing both for herself just as he is. Drawing closer to God is the answer, following the example of Christ is the answer. Let no husband blame his wife for the actions and choices he makes.

God to Adam, did you eat of the tree which I commanded you not to eat. Adam to God, the woman you gave to be with me she gave me of the tree and I did eat. It is as ineffectual an answer today as when it was first stated. God will hold you responsible for your actions. The battle for your marriage is raging, the enemy is advancing, soldier of Christ will you put your armor on or will you like too many others, walk off of the battlefield?

11

WHAT SHE MEANS WHEN SHE SAYS, "YOU DON'T LOVE ME"

It is axiomatic that every wife wants to be loved by her husband. And I would argue that most every husband wants to love his wife. I'm sure you are trying in whatever way you understand it. Like reverence, (which will be discussed in her section) she knows she deserves love, but she may have a hard time communicating what should be so basic a thing to receive. She knows it is not difficult to understand what the Lord said.

> Husbands, love your wives, as Christ loved the church and gave himself up for her, that he might sanctify her, having cleansed her by the washing of water with the word, so that he might present the church to himself in splendor, without spot or wrinkle or any such thing, that she might be holy and without blemish. In the same way husbands should love their wives as their own bodies. He who loves his wife loves himself.
>
> -Ephesians 5:25-28

It is so hard to feel the need to convince someone to give you something that you believe is so basic to your existence. A son honors a father, and in that vein a husband loves his wife. And when a wife does not feel loved, it is enough to drive her crazy. The best she can muster sometimes is to simply blurt out in frustration, "You don't love me."

If you have ever heard that phrase knows that arguing is not the answer, defending yourself never works, and asking, "Well, what do you want from me?" provides no tangible benefit. Just what does she mean? Let's learn from the first woman on earth and give to our wives what Eve had. If you do, you will never again hear those four dreaded words, "you don't love me."

Eve Had Preeminence

When Adam awoke from his slumber and God brought Eve before him, Eve had what every woman wants from her husband. She was his only focus; she had no rival for his attention. The same could be said for Christ and the church. The church is preeminent in the mind of Christ. Your wife can be made to feel as if she is competing for the number-one place in your life. This is a space she thought she had when she married you; it's actually *why* she said yes to your proposal.

Her competition can include work, play, friends, family, hobbies, and children. We give our time to what is important to us. Wives often feel like they lose the battle to one or more of these other things. The wise Solomon said to everything there is a time and a season. There is a time for work, play, family, and friends. But your wife must be first and the highest priority in your life. Google's dictionary says of preeminence that it is the "fact of surpassing all others; superiority." Her concept of love is that, as your wife, she will be preeminent. To this she has a right, and she is not being difficult for desiring it. Every wife wants to be preeminent in her husbands life.

Eve Had Adam's Attention

Your wife wants you to pay attention to her. Eve had this in spades from Adam; his first words prove it: "This is now bone of my bones and flesh of my flesh." Likewise, the church had our Lord's attention. Christ was singularly focused on the church (Matt. 16:18); not even the gates of hell would prevent him from building her. Adam was focused on Eve, and every wife wants her husband to focus his attention on her.

The competition for a man's focus is fierce; just check the calendar and see what season it is. Husbands look forward to making their wives widows during sports seasons. It's football season, and she already knows what happens. "I've got to work out"; "The boys need me"; "I need to do this thing or that thing." A man's focus and attention can be everywhere but on his wife if he is not careful.

No one ever enjoys being an afterthought; just break the word up to appreciate how serious it is. The word means "I thought of you after my other thought. There was a first thought; you were not it. Something happened or some time elapsed, and then I thought about you afterward." Wow! Your wife will not feel loved if she is an afterthought. She desires to be the focus of your life and have the attention of her husband? She deserves your attention, and asking for it is troublesome and difficult for her because she shouldn't have to. You vowed your undying love and devotion to her, she believed you.

Eve Had Adam's Approval
Adam approved of Eve, and Christ approves of his church. When Adam saw her, he said "now" or "at last." Eve was sufficient, and Adam told her that. If women are challenged with anything today, it is trying to obtain and sustain the approval of their husbands.

She desires so strongly that you would have eyes only for her. She would love to know that you are satisfied with her love, her shape, her house, and her cooking. You must be the one to assure her through words and deeds that you don't want anyone or anything more than her. She wants assurance that she is all that you need and want. She wants to know that she meets and satisfies all of your desires and needs.

If men fall down anywhere, it is here. From nearly as far back as she can remember, your wife has been concerned about her physical body. It has been ingrained into her, and unfortunately has become a part of her. Movies, magazines, commercials, videos, and every form of media tell her one thing—you are not as you ought to be, no matter what she is.

Lose more weight; get fitter; show more cleavage; get more cleavage to show. Eat this, do that, wear this, buy that, walk like this, talk like that, do your hair this way. Her whole life has been saturated and inundated with never being good enough. She said yes to your proposal because you convinced her she was sufficient just as she was. You courted her, spoke kind beautiful words to her, demonstrated your care, bought her gifts and pledged your undying love to her. At last she had someone who loved her just for her. You have no idea what a horrible and sad time it is for her when you begin to show her you have changed your mind.

The wise Solomon gave men this instruction, and every man should keep this wisdom before him:

> Drink water from your own cistern, flowing water from your own well. Should your springs be scattered abroad, streams of water in the streets? Let them be for yourself alone, and not for strangers with you. Let your fountain be blessed, and rejoice in the wife of your youth, a lovely deer, a graceful doe. Let her breasts fill you at all times with delight; be intoxicated always in her love. Why should you be intoxicated, my son, with a forbidden woman and embrace the bosom of an adulteress?
>
> —Proverbs 5:15–20

Every woman wants to be sufficient for her husband. So, if you give other women, pornography, and anything else a place in your heart you will hurt your wife. The hurt will be so great that she might just say, "you don't love me."

Eve Was One with Adam
Eve woke up, walked into the garden, and stood before Adam. He took one look and said, "This is now bone of my bones and flesh of my flesh." She was from his body, and she was one with him. In the

same way, scripture informs us that, as Christians, we are members of Christ's body. This great mystery of Christ and his church was based on the original couple. Eve was a member of Adam's body.

Marriage is about oneness; it is about being united. Every wife desires to be one with her husband. No wife desires to get married and remain single. She understands that two have become one. She doesn't want her own life anymore; that's why she is getting married. She doesn't want to be separated, left apart, or alone. Women know well, "I can do bad all by myself."

Any man getting married needs to understand his wife's desire, and he should want the same thing. She is not giving her life so her husband can remain a bachelor. To love her, you must glue yourself to her. This will enable you to write a new story with your wife. In marriage, *I, mine,* and *my* give way to *we, ours,* and *us.* Married life should be described in terms of *our* story.

What are we going to do? How are we going to prepare for the future? Where will we live, and how will we rear our children? No wife wants two; she wants two to become one. Adam was one with Eve, and Christ is one with the church. When a wife uses the word *love,* she means she wants to be one with her husband. If you are not one with her, she will say, "you don't love me."

Adam Cared For Eve
Adam's care for Eve is seen immediately in his announcement of her relationship to him. She was bone of his bones and flesh of his flesh. When Paul penned Ephesians 5, he helped us understand that care. The care is evident because no man ever hated his own flesh but nourishes it and cherishes it.

We don't have to wonder what life was like for Adam and Eve because Christ's care for the church was the same care. The nourishing and cherishing is done for a wife even as Christ does for the church. Every wife wants to be cared about and asked how she's doing. When a husband asks his wife about her state of being, her health, and her mood, this care for her evidences his love for her.

A man's wife wants to be cared for—"Honey, what do you need?" "Sure, babe, how can I help you?" Your wife will struggle to understand that she is loved if she feels that you aren't interested in her wellbeing. "Do I matter?" will be the thing she asks herself. "Does he care about me, my wants, needs, and desires?" If your wife doubts that she is nourished and cherished, she will doubt that she is loved.

Eve Was Cared Over

Admittedly it is a strange heading, but all it means is this: a woman who is married is clear in her mind that she will be cared for over everyone else in the world. Simply put, she will be first in order of importance in her husband's life. The words of Genesis 2:24 were spoken by God: "Therefore shall a man leave his father and mother and shall cleave unto his wife." This sentiment is very well understood by your wife.

When it comes to your family, friends, mother, father, sisters, and brothers, she does not want to take second place. While all of those relationships are important and they will remain, marriage is unique and excels over them all. She needs you to be her champion to all of the other people in you life. A husband will make a huge mistake if he tries to try to walk the line between both and please everyone.

When he is with his family, he will try to maintain the same relationships and actions they had before marriage. This is unsustainable because he is married; yet those in the family often continue to want the same level of care from him. His wife should naturally be his priority, but he doesn't want to hurt his family by telling them no. Instead, he tells his wife to be understanding, patient, and to just go with it.

If she doesn't and raises concerns about it, then he chides her for not understanding. Or when he is with them, he throws her under the bus with statements like, "I would, but she doesn't want to," or, "No, we can't; my wife doesn't want to." These actions paint his wife as the bad guy—while he remains the good guy. Such action allows his family to feel justified in their ugliness toward her.

Such action on the part of any husband will have his wife wondering if he loves her. If he did love her, then he would emulate Christ's love for his church. The Lord cared for his church above all else; he spoke of it as being his meat to eat (John 4:31–34). His care is evidenced in that he gave his life to purchase the church (Acts 20:28). When a woman questions her husband's love for her, he should know that she desires to be cared for over everyone else in his life.

One Word to Capture It All—Regard
Do you regard her? The word *regard* means "to attend to with respect and estimation; to value; to attend to as a thing that affects our interest or happiness; to fix the mind on as a matter of importance. To esteem; to hold in respect and affection." (e-sword.com).

These definitions express well how Christ behaved toward the church. He regarded her, attended to her, and fixed his mind on her. To appreciate Christ's regard for the church, read this passage:

> And to bring to light for everyone what is the plan of the mystery hidden for ages in God who created all things, so that through the church the manifold wisdom of God might now be made known to the rulers and authorities in the heavenly places. This was according to the eternal purpose that he has realized in Christ Jesus our Lord.
>
> —Ephesians 3:9–11

The context of the passage is the mystery of God revealed to his apostles and prophets. The mystery is explained in Ephesians 3:6. It is that Christ would come and reconcile all men unto God in one body. Ephesians 1:22–23 explains that the body is the church. Ephesians 2:13–16 tells us that Christ is the one who reconciles all men into one body. Ephesians 4:4–6 tells us that there is one body, and Ephesians 5:23–25 informs us that Christ is the Savior of the body.

With all of that in mind, we should realize that the passages above help us appreciate when Christ and God had this plan in mind. The plan was in God's mind, and he made it known. The time is revealed in these words: *it was according to the eternal purpose of God realized in Jesus Christ.* How did Christ regard the church? It was his singular mission, and it was purposed in eternity. His death on the cross was the expression of an eternal idea.

How does regard look practically? When you regard your wife, that regard for her impacts your decisions about her. The decisions you make range from the mundane to the major. Those decisions will impact your wife's and children's lives. Her life is in your hands spiritually, physically, emotionally, and mentally. She trusted you and voluntarily placed her heart and life in your hands.

Regarding her means she is on your mind. She is no afterthought; she is the forethought. A man who regards his wife wouldn't do things without considering the cost to her. For wives, the word *love* has the word *regard* stuffed inside. Anytime she questions your love for her, what she is saying is that she does not believe, feel, or think that you regard her. She will determine this based on what you do and say. If she is regarded she should know it because their should be evidence. Jesus said we could know people by their fruit. The fruit on our life tree, reveals our heart.

Influence
It should not be a woman's desire to tell her husband what to do. But she should have some influence with him. If your wife shares her pain, expresses her concern or sadness about something you are do-ing. She will want to know that her words matter. They will if she has any influence with you. You must let her know that her feelings matter because she is regarded. You can't simply say, "I love you" and live something else. You must be willing to move for her, listen to her concerns, and value her input. That regard and care will help her to know that she can influence him.

Unfortunately, she may be no better at expressing the love she desires than he is at expressing the reverence he craves, so it may come out combatively. She just wants to know that she matters, that he cares, and that she is his first priority. That doesn't mean she will always get her way. But if she can never have her way or know that she matters, then she will believe that she is not loved, and she might just be right.

None of the above is wrong for her to desire, and nothing herein stated shows a problem on her part. She doesn't want pity or patronization; she wants to be loved. You promised her that you loved her, and she believed you. The treatment you gave her in dating was so good and your regard for her so evident that she said yes to marriage.

She said yes to being loved like you showed her when you were dating. She said yes to being loved like Christ loved the church. The God who made you both told husbands to love their wives. The Christ who came and died for us showed us what love is, and he said to love your wife as he loved the church. If you are a husband, you said you loved her, so show it. Christ said to love her, so she cannot be wrong for wanting you to do it. Husband's let each of you love your wife is from God not women. Make a commitment to love your wife like Christ loved the church.

When she says, "You don't love me," this is what she means, you have to answer if she is right.

SECTION 3

Chapters 12-16

The Church Christ's Bride - A Wife's Example

For Her

12

GOD CARES FOR WOMEN

Sadly, it did not take long for man to abuse God's design of male leadership. We do not read very far into scripture before we see this occurring. Genesis 4:19 records, "And Lamech took two wives. The name of the one was Adah, and the name of the other Zillah." How sad that by Genesis 4, men were already taking multiple wives.

This was contrary to God's directive of leaving one's father and mother and cleaving unto his wife, not wives. The abuse of men toward women continued and increasingly grew worse. By the time of Noah, things had become so bad that God judged the world with a flood. Among the many sins being committed was the mistreatment of women: "When man began to multiply on the face of the land and daughters were born to them, the sons of God saw that the daughters of man were attractive. And they took as their wives any they chose" (Gen. 6:1–2).

While the flood destroyed the world, the nature of man did not change. Noah left the ark and got drunk (Gen. 9:20–21). The abuse of women also resumed as men spread over the earth. The practice was so commonplace that when God chose Israel, he gave laws to protect women against further abuse.

A Bill of Divorcement

Being divorced hardly seems like something to help women, but God's law concerning it was. The men were not writing bills of divorcement. It seems they were simply getting rid of their wives on any whim. God does not sanction the evil of man. Men were already doing evil, and God often regulated the behavior they persisted in doing. Deuteronomy 24:1–4 is one case in point.

> When a man takes a wife and marries her, if then she finds no favor in his eyes because he has found some indecency in her, and he writes her a certificate of divorce and puts it in her hand and sends her out of his house, and she departs out of his house, and if she goes and becomes another man's wife, and the latter man hates her and writes her a certificate of divorce and puts it in her hand and sends her out of his house, or if the latter man dies, who took her to be his wife, then her former husband, who sent her away, may not take her again to be his wife, after she has been defiled, for that is an abomination before the LORD. And you shall not bring sin upon the land that the LORD your God is giving you for an inheritance.

In Israel, God Made Provisions to Protect Women

If the husband found some uncleanness in her, he could write her a bill of divorcement. But once he put her away, she could go and marry again. But he could not marry her again.

The Pharisees' Q&A with Jesus Proves Their Understanding

Matthew records that the Pharisees approached Jesus as they often did, "tempting him." Their question to the Lord revolves around divorcing their wives. Their intention is to put Christ at odds with their teachers or Moses. Either way, they would have great opportunity to accuse him.

The Lord's answer and the subsequent discussion evidence God's care for women and man's desire to take advantage of them.

And Pharisees came up to him and tested him by asking, "Is it lawful to divorce one's wife for any cause?" He answered, "Have you not read that he who created them from the beginning made them male and female, and said, 'Therefore a man shall leave his father and his mother and hold fast to his wife, and the two shall become one flesh'? So they are no longer two but one flesh. What therefore God has joined together, let not man separate."

—Matthew 19:3–6

Jesus answered their question by noting God's intention from the beginning. His answer appeals to God's design and intended function. It manifests God's care for women. The one who made them at the beginning intended the man to marry a woman and remain glued to her for life. Genesis 2 does not give any cause for divorce because what God joined together, man was never intended to put asunder.

Man's Hard Heart

Disappointed with the answer, the Pharisees continued with their questions. Their question and the Lord's answer are telling.

They said to him, "Why then did Moses command one to give a certificate of divorce and to send her away?" He said to them, "Because of your hardness of heart Moses allowed you to divorce your wives, but from the beginning it was not so."

—Matthew 19:7–8

What is clear from this interchange is that God's design does not demand or sanction men abusing women. The command of God to his people is specifically given to negate the abuse that is sadly already present in the life of his people. Their hard hearts made this provision necessary, not God's design. Jesus affirmed the design from the beginning. Adam couldn't marry more than one woman because only one was given. I don't know of a single verse that says Adam ever did.

No women should know the pain, hurt, and mistreatment of being put away for another woman or any careless, restless thought of her husband. The designer never intended his design to function in such a manner. Men do not have God's approval to grow tired of their wives and seek a new model. God cares for women, and men should too.

Christ Elevated Women

The gospel of Jesus Christ exalts women to equality with men like no other system of faith ever has. In the first-century world, the gospel message of equality would have been unheard of and disbelieved based solely on its teaching of the equality of men and women before God.

For as many of you as were baptized into Christ have put on Christ. There is neither Jew nor Greek, there is neither slave nor free, there is no male and female, for you are all one in Christ Jesus.

—Galatians 3:27–28

That the gospel is under discussion cannot reasonably be argued. The entire book of Galatians is about the gospel of Christ that saves (Gal. 1:6–9; 5:4). Before God, there is no distinction between gender, ethnicity, social status, or any other thing. Women are created in the image of God, just as men are. That this means that men and women have the same role, however, is untrue. The gospel did not change the design of marriage. There are different roles and functions for believers.

For those who disagree, please consider that a young person who becomes a Christian is still subject to his parents (Eph. 6:1–2). But if being a Christian removes distinction in roles, he is no longer subject to his parents. If equality in salvation removes all distinctions, parents and children in Christ are simply spiritual siblings. The child can rightly say to his parents that no one is over anyone. We are all one in Christ, so let's dispense with the roles of parent and child. The same could be said of employees and bosses. The employee should not go to work with his Christian boss and announce, "Because of Christ, we now have no role difference in our relationship."

Husbands, love your wives, as Christ loved the church and gave himself up for her.

—Ephesians 5:25

No husband can do more for his wife than to love her as Christ loves the church. Loving one's wife per the example of Christ will never lend itself to abuse. The charge is to love her to the point of being willing to die for her. The gospel of Christ exalts our thoughts and treatment of women. Men and women are blessed if we follow the teachings of Christ.

In the same way husbands should love their wives as their own bodies. He who loves his wife loves himself. For no one ever hated his own flesh, but nourishes and cherishes it, just as Christ does the church.

—Ephesians 5:28–29

No abuse would ever happen to women if husbands loved their wives as Christ loved the church and as they loved themselves. Let it be understood that the design of God demonstrates care for women; the gospel of Christ exalts women. But men have turned away from God and, under the guise of God's plan, have abused women. God's instructions to women are also given to protect them.

God Said to Get Married and Then Have Sex
Given the fact that men have exploited and continue to exploit, mistreat, and abuse women, this instruction from God ought to be of great interest to women. Why would God instruct us to wait until marriage to have sex? To ask is to answer, isn't it? If he is not willing to marry you then don't have sex with him.

Keep Yourself until Marriage
If a man will please God (women too), he cannot have sex before marriage. Such action is unrighteous, and those who persist in sin cannot go to heaven. Or do you not know that the unrighteous will not inherit the kingdom of God? Do not be deceived: neither the sexually immoral, nor idolaters, nor adulterers, nor men who practice homosexuality (1 Cor. 6:9).

If women have a built-in protection against abuse and mistreatment by men, then keeping themselves pure is among the surest ways to do so. But as long as women are willing to have sex before marriage, they open themselves up to potential mistreatment. Many a man is willing to have sex with any woman who will without the commitment of marriage.

This proverb is true: why buy the cow if you can have the milk for free? Of course, even this instruction for a woman's good is met with opposition. Human wisdom says nothing is wrong with sex before marriage. Some even think that there is nothing wrong with sex on the first date. Others move the line from first to third or fifth. The suggestion of ninety days, made by one popular author, is thought to be extreme.

God says wait until marriage. Men and women should wait until they are married to have sex. A young lady will be told that the boy or man loves her. She will hear how beautiful she is and how he cannot live without her—until at last he has sex with her, and then suddenly he can live without her, and soon he does and it is on to the next girl.

In response to this terrible treatment, many people think it is a good idea to tell women to behave the same way. If men can be dogs, then why can't women? Reading the words should evidence the sad conclusion of the suggestion. If men are bad, mean, and evil people for treating women in such a fashion, how can the solution be for women to become bad, mean, and evil people to fix the problem.

You are not responsible for fixing the world. You need to work on your own life. It is not a matter of what men and women do. It is a matter of what you do or will do. It is not a good idea for women to be promiscuous—but men shouldn't be either. As parents of a bygone era used to say, if everybody was jumping off the bridge, would you jump to?

Counting the Cost

It would be difficult to estimate the number of girls/women who have been hurt, both emotionally and physically, by boys/men after having pre-marital sex with them. Generally women need to be emotionally attached before they will have sex with a man. Once attached girls and women run after the guy; often feeling like she has to have him. In this situation she is willing to forgo Daddy and Mama, sister and brother, and even God if it means having him.

That same guy will continue to have sex with her as long as she allows. He may even get her pregnant and leave her with the baby. If she can, she will return to the same people who warned her against the guy—and she will be returning with a baby and maybe a hatred for males. Such treatment from men cause women to suffer mentally, emotionally, and possibly even physically.

Her troubles will continue because guys will not stop. Another guy will come along and see her with her child. He will know she is or has been sexually active and assume that she is easy to have sex with and he will try. Young ladies often find themselves in what seems like an impossible situation. Men will have them for their bodies and nothing else, but being alone with no one to love doesn't seem like a viable option either.

Some women with children do find good men who are willing to marry them and do right. While other women feel compelled to settle for knuckleheads, believing themselves to be damaged goods. A man using a woman for her body harms a woman's estimation of her self-worth. Though it is rarely spoken of, treating women in this way hurts him mentally and emotionally as well.

Then there are those men who have decided, despite their own lives, "I am not marrying a woman with a child." These men care little for the carnage to women they have left in their wake. Men talk about "girls to date" and "girls to marry." The ones who give them sex before marriage are for dating. The ones who say no and think highly of God and themselves are worth marrying. Yes, sadly some men think this way and say these things out loud.

The solution and safety for women against the evil of men is to follow God's words. Keep yourself until you're married. If he does love you, then let him marry you. Don't give the cookie without getting the commitment. If he won't marry you without having sex first then keep looking and let him go and find someone else. If he can have sex with you before marriage, you will be one of those women for dating not marriage. You must not think of men as projects for you to fix and save. God does the fixing and Jesus does the saving, he needs Jesus not your body. A clear indication of that is he is asking for your body before marriage, yes he needs Jesus.

God Told Men to Love, Honor, and Cherish Women
There is certainly a lot of pressure on women, but wouldn't women prefer to be in charge of their choices rather than others? Men are not instructed to put up with, bear, or deal with women. They are told to love, honor, and cherish them. But we can't ask others to do for us what we are unwilling to do for ourselves.

Love, Honor, and Cherish Yourself
Women really must evaluate who is on their side and who is their enemy. Are the people teaching you to expose your body and shake your groove thing really your friends? Men and women exploit women for money, power, and fame. Some ads exploiting women are created, shot, and run by women. What are the "hot" female artists singing to you? What are they telling you to do? Is it the same as what Jesus is telling you to do? We know well what the male artists are singing, and telling you to do. You can't show off your bass and then tell men to listen to your brain.

The question is how are representing yourself, not how you rep someone else's brands or ideas. Are the ways you dress, talk, walk, and live reflective of one who loves, honors, and cherishes God and herself? You should think it difficult to ask men to do for you what you are unwilling to do for yourself. Especially since you know how many men act already. History is clear, ungodly men will take advantage of women if allowed an opportunity.

It is a profoundly consistent thing in life. Men treat women the way women present themselves to men. Let us not pretend. If you expose all of your physical beauty, men will look at it and think you intend for them to respond to it. If I see someone dressed up in big red shoes with a curly, multicolored wig and a big red nose, you will forgive me if I think he should tell jokes, make balloon animals, and provide entertainment for children. I would make the mistake of believing a person so dressed was a clown.

If you wear tight, form-fitting clothes, low-cut dresses, high skirts, pounds of makeup, stilts for shoes, men might approach you believing you want to be so treated. Regardless of how any woman dresses, however, no one should ever touch her without her permission. Certainly no one should ever assault her, and no means no. Victims should not be blamed because of the evil of criminals.

Still, the world, ads, commercials, and nearly all of media show women with as little on as possible. Girls and women are led to believe they must expose themselves to make it. Unfortunately, boys and men are getting the same messages and they to believe them. The people who claim to help women end up exploiting women through their messages. "Get hard, cold and tough like men," women are told. Or, "sleep around like men." "Show off your body; you got it, so flaunt it." Sometimes girls are given this bad advice by women. None of this will help or has ever helped women.

God Cares for Women

Man's abuse does not cast reflection on God's design, it manifests man's hard heart. God cares for women, so he exalts them and commands men to do the same. Any man who will follow God must think as highly as women as God does. He demands that husbands cherish and nourish their wives.

Women, you should look around the world and ask yourself if it is a good idea for me to be sexually active before marriage. If you will please God, the answer is no. That decision will help you in your life and in your future marriage. Men shouldn't sin by being sexually active either. But many men have no problem using a double standard on women, maybe you have noticed.

The responsibility for the outcome of our lives is largely in our hands. Knowing what women know about men, how can anyone think it is a good idea to sleep with them before marriage? Don't give yourself to a man without the high commitment of marriage. You are worth infinitely more than a few smooth lines, dinner, and a movie. You are infinitely stronger than accepting sin and poor treatment because of the threat of being alone.

As a woman, God loves you and made you in his image. Therefore, God says you should love, honor, and cherish yourself. Before you learn to love a man, learn to love yourself.

I tell women all the time, "God made man the head, but he lets you choose who gets the job." Don't hire a lazy, shiftless, no-good man to be the head of your life, be very selective in your hiring process.

God cares for you; make sure you care for yourself?

13

WHY GOD GAVE LEADERSHIP

Those who follow are not slaves to those who lead. In the Bible, whenever God put someone in authority over another person or group of people, he always empowered that person to carry out his commands. Those people led with God's authority behind them (Exod. 19:6–9). Therefore, to disobey them was to disobey God, as the following indicates.

- To despise Moses was to despise God (Heb. 10:28).
- The government is ordained by God (Rom. 13:1–2).
- The eldership is ordained by God (Acts 20:28).
- Parents are in the position of God (Eph. 6:1–3).
- Husbands are in the position of Christ (Eph. 5:23–24).

Those who lead are not held hostage to those who follow; they are only hostage to God.

The counterpoint is this: those who follow are not slaves to those who lead; they are only slaves to God. This brings to mind a scary situation for those who follow. If someone is over me, what if they take advantage of his or her position? If Moses leads Israel, what would happen if Moses took advantage of his position? If the government rules over its citizens, what if the government abuses its power? If an eldership is over the members, what if they lord it over God's heritage? If parents are over children, what if they abuse their babies?

In light of all that has been said, a woman who is married and trying to live a godly life may wonder what happens if her husband abuses his position, abuses her, or just does not do right by her. It is natural for anyone who is led in any circumstance to be so concerned, and it is reasonable for women to be so concerned, especially since history is replete with abuse in every one of these dynamics. Israel's leaders did abuse God's people; governments have abused citizens; elders arose and abused the church (Acts 20:29–31); masters abused servants; parents abused children; and some husbands have abused their wives.

The fact that abuse existed and still persists is undeniable. This may be the reason many are opposed to the arrangement. Given our belief in the infinite knowledge of God, we must know that he knew of the potential for abuse. Still, he designed the roles the way he did, so we should ask ourselves why. Why would God do things the way he did? In other words, why is there leadership at all?

Both leaders and followers must understand why God arranged things the way he did. If we understand why God gave leadership, the animosity, suspicion, and distrust would disappear. Husbands and wives would enjoy their roles and find comfort and joy in God. The joy and comfort is not in a husband's flawless execution of the role.

The joy and comfort is in the God who created the people, provided the marriage, and gave the commands for them to live in the roles. Joy is always found in God. Israel could always rejoice in the God who delivered them, but not always in the leaders who led them.

Part of the explanation of leadership is this: God never intended to always have direct contact with his people. However, he did want his people to be cared for the way he would care for them. So God devised representative leadership; hence, *the leader represents God!*

The benefits of leadership are for God's people. One benefit is they would never be alone. God, through his leader, would always be with them. Another benefit is his people would never be ignorant of him because God would instruct the leader, and the leader would teach the people of God. Finally, his people's needs would be met. As we will notice later, every leader is to provide something for those he leads. In this way, through the leader, God could care for his people.

If we change our thoughts about the arrangement for both leaders and followers, we will enjoy the rich blessings God has given us through representative leadership. Let's consider why God designed leadership.

God's Care for His People

The burning bush is one of the more memorable accounts in scripture. Moses saw a bush on fire but not consumed. He approached the bush to see why the bush wasn't burnt, and a voice spoke to him out of the bush. If the first part was interesting, it is hard to imagine what Moses was thinking after the voice spoke. He was told to take off his shoes because the ground he was standing on was holy. Being in God's presence is always a holy occasion. God introduced himself to Moses as the God of his fathers, the God of Abraham, Isaac, and Jacob.

Here is where the point begins to be made. God called Moses and chose him to go and deliver Israel from slavery in Egypt. Let's read the text and then discuss the point.

> And the LORD said, I have surely seen the affliction of my people which are in Egypt, and have heard their cry by reason of their taskmasters; for I know their sorrows; And I am come down to deliver them out of the hand of the Egyptians, and to bring them up out of that land unto a good land and a large, unto a land flowing with milk and honey; unto the place of the Canaanites, and the Hittites, and the Amorites, and the Perizzites, and the Hivites, and the Jebusites. Now therefore, behold, the cry of the children of Israel is come unto me: and I have also seen the oppression wherewith the Egyptians oppress them. Come now therefore, and I will send thee unto Pharaoh, that thou

mayest bring forth my people the children of Israel out of Egypt.

—Exodus 3:7–10

God's care for his people is a driving force behind his provision of leaders. Those who lead must know they represent God, and those who are led are to be comforted by their place in God's heart.

Why did God Call Moses? Read again the exact same text, but this time notice the italicized portions.

> And the LORD said, *I have surely seen the affliction of my people* which are in Egypt, and have *heard their cry* by reason of their taskmasters; for *I know their sorrows*; And *I am come down to deliver them* out of the hand of the Egyptians, and *to bring them up out* of that land unto a good land and a large, unto a land flowing with milk and honey; unto the place of the Canaanites, and the Hittites, and the Amorites, and the Perizzites, and the Hivites, and the Jebusites. Now therefore, behold, *the cry of the children of Israel is come unto me*: and *I have also seen the oppression* where-with the Egyptians oppress them. Come now there-fore, and *I will send thee* unto Pharaoh, that thou mayest *bring forth my people* the children of Israel out of Egypt.

If you were asked, "Why did God send Moses to lead Israel?" what would you say? These passages make it clear that God saw his people's suffering, and he was going to relieve them. Therefore, he sent Moses to bring his people out so he could take them into a land flowing with milk and honey.

God's care for his people is why he called Moses to lead Israel. It was not about Moses; it was about God's love for his people. Leadership is never about the leader; it is about the God who called him to lead. Both leaders and followers must learn this.

God's Solutions to His People's Problem

In every arena of godly leadership, leaders are to be problem solvers and peace providers for God's people, because God desires his people to be at peace and he is not pleased when his people are scattered and shattered. Neither is God pleased when his people are agitated and irritated. This is not the way God would lead his people.

David may have said it best: "The LORD is my shepherd; I shall not want. He maketh me to lie down in green pastures: he leadeth me beside the still waters" (Psalm 23:1–2).

Green pastures indicate provision, and still waters indicate peace. It is said that sheep will not eat or drink unless they feel safe and secure. Leaders in Israel and the church were put in place to alleviate the problems of the people. The people of Israel came to Moses all day and night to present their cases before him so he could judge them (Exod. 18:13–20). Jethro watched and told Moses that what he was doing was not good and that if he continued, he would wear himself out.

His solution for Moses was to get other able men to help him; the men were to help Moses and provide solutions to the people's problems.

> Moreover, look for able men from all the people, men who fear God, who are trustworthy and hate a bribe, and place such men over the people as chiefs of thousands, of hundreds, of fifties, and of tens. And let them judge the people at all times. Every great matter they shall bring to you, but any small matter they shall decide themselves. So it will be easier for you, and they will bear the burden with you. If you do this, God will direct you, you will be able to endure, and all this people also will go to their place in peace.

> —Exodus 18:21–23 KJV

It is exciting to consider that the leaders were put in place to provide solutions for God's people and to bring peace to their lives. The same can be seen in the early church when problems were encountered (Acts 6:1–5).

God's Protection for His People

God desires the wellbeing and safety of his people. In the Old Testament, Moses, Joshua, the judges, and the kings protected God's people. The wars were physical and the defense of God's people tantamount. In Christ, the leaders are charged with the spiritual protection of his people. Elders are charged with the spiritual welfare of God's flock.

> Pay careful attention to yourselves and to all the flock, in which the Holy Spirit has made you overseers, to care for the church of God, which he obtained with his own blood. I know that after my departure fierce wolves will come in among you, not sparing the flock; and from among your own selves will arise men speaking twisted things, to draw away the disciples after them. Therefore be alert, remembering that for three years I did not cease night or day to admonish everyone with tears. And now I commend you to God and to the word of his grace, which is able to build you up and to give you the inheritance among all those who are sanctified.
>
> —Acts 20:28–32

Those who shepherd God's people are charged by God to protect the spiritual wellbeing of his people. Shepherds are to protect them from false teachers and false doctrine. They are to teach God's Word faithfully and ensure that those they allow to preach to them do the same.

God's Provision for His People

Every leader was to provide something for God's people. Moses provided Israel with God's Word, direction, and instruction. Government is to provide protection and safety for God's people (Rom. 13:3–4). Elders are to feed, lead, and retrieve God's people (Acts 20:28; Luke 15:3-5). Parents are to provide a godly example, instruction in God's Word, discipline, and correction for their children (Deut. 6:7–10; Eph. 6:4; 2 Tim. 3:15). A husband is to provide for his wife and for those of his household (1 Tim. 5:8).

Husbands Are God's Leaders

A husband is hardly an arbitrary, power-hungry dictator. He must never think of his wife as his slave or a possession he owns. Instead, she is precious and cared for by the God of heaven. The leadership of her husband is because God desires to be connected to her and care for her. The arrangement is how God interacts through representation with his people. Her husband is God's representative leader, and her greatest ally is God.

Leaders' harshest critics will not be members under elders, citizens under governments, employees under bosses, children under parents, or wives under husbands. The one looking most intently at the job being done is the one who designed the role and is being represented, and that is God! Our marriages will improve if we know why God has leaders in the first place.

Husbands are to care for their wives as God would care for his child. God expects her husband to be a problem solver and peace provider for her life. To that end, every wife must understand that this is why, when she comes home with a problem, her husband listens and then offers solutions. He is designed to feel the weight of solving problems. When she hurts, he hurts; when she is upset, he is upset; and when she is irritated, he is irritated at whoever is irritating her.

So when she comes home and tells him about the day she had and the people who are stressing her life, she should not be surprised that her husband gives her specific solutions to solve the issue. He is amazed when he learns that the talk on Monday with her about those harsh people at work wasn't intended to be solved, just heard, and that on Tuesday, he should pull up a chair to listen to how terribly his wife is being treated and how bad she feels, but he is to understand that her pain and stress actually need no solution. She simply needs to be heard. And then on Wednesday he should look forward to hearing it again. The woman he pledged his love and life to is hurting. The woman he loves and will die for is in pain. Who told us men should be all right with just listening to it and not wanting to stop it?

All wives need to know that God made him this way. He represents God, and one of God's children is in need. No one can imagine God just listening. When God heard his people crying he told Moses to go and deliver them.

> Then the Lord said, "I have surely seen the affliction of my people who are in Egypt and have heard their cry because of their taskmasters. I know their sufferings, and I have come down to deliver them out of the hand of the Egyptians and to bring them up out of that land to a good and broad land, a land flowing with milk and honey, to the place of the Canaanites, the Hittites, the Amorites, the Perizzites, the Hivites, and the Jebusites. And now, behold, the cry of the people of Israel has come to me, and I have also seen the oppression with which the Egyptians oppress them. Come, I will send you to Pharaoh that you may bring my people, the children of Israel, out of Egypt."
>
> -Exodus 3:7-10

The husband who regards his wife will want to help his wife. So don't be angry at your husband if he wants to help solve his wife's problems. He is simply doing what God would do. He will protect her physically should a need arise and even be willing to lay down his life for her. But he especially protects her spiritually by living for God himself and leading her to do the same. Every husband is to provide for his wife's needs in God's stead. And he should love her as Christ loved the church.

The husband who understands why God designed leadership will feel the privilege, power, and weight of standing in the stead of God. He will strive to love and cares for his wife the way God cares for his people. When a wife understands why God designed things the way he did, she will feel the great care of being on God's mind. This knowledge will comfort her heart, assure her mind, and evoke trust in the God her husband represents.

For as many abusers as there have been, we have a Bible and a history full of people who did as God desired. Moses, Joshua, and a host of others led Israel as God desired. They were not perfect, but they were faithful. Many elders have been faithful to God's charge, and congregations have been blessed. Numerous parents have represented God faithfully in their homes. And there have been and are many husbands who have represented God faithfully toward their wives. For those who have, their wives will be the first to tell you what a blessing their leadership was to their lives.

If it is questioned whether a woman is connected to God without a husband, she is. No woman needs a man to commune with God. The risen Christ, her Savior, is all she needs to get to God. So no single woman need be concerned about this chapter and the connection it makes between the role of husbands and their wives. Every wife has her own relationship with God and is accountable to God for her soul.

There are two roles we can enter as humans that provide aspects of a relationship with God that cannot be had any other way. One way is parenting. When one becomes a parent, loving a child goes from theory and concept to reality. When God refers to us as his children, parents can relate to that in a way single people can't. You have to have one of those special little people to know. It doesn't mean single people aren't connected to God. But you can't know what it is like to have a child if you don't have one.

The second way is marriage. No other relationship is like it. God refers to us as his bride. No husband is without the idea of what that means. A single man can have dates and girlfriends. He can even say he loves them. But that is not marriage, and those women are not his wife. Every husband who has stood and watched her walk down the aisle knows. He sees God's actions toward his people, and he knows what it means to be married. In this connection, his role is to represent God. He is all in, laying down his life. And for his wife and children, he will. God would have nothing less, for he laid down his life for his bride.

14

GOD'S WORD TO THOSE WHO FOLLOW

I n trying to understand the mind of God, the beginning is often the best place to start. The beginning of the home is recorded for us in Genesis 2:18–25. The genesis of Moses's leadership in Israel is recorded in Exodus 3. The things we learn in the text are crucial to the success of those who follow God-ordained leadership.

If those who lead should read Genesis 2 anew, then those who follow should read Exodus 3 anew. Like leaders, they will get a clearer understanding of the follower's role and responsibility toward God. Moses's call and leadership will help us in understanding our *followship*.

God Arranged the Relationship

God's Purpose Was Being Fulfilled
God met Moses at the burning bush and told Moses of the plight of his people and his desire to deliver them.

> Then the LORD said, "I have surely seen the affliction of my people who are in Egypt and have heard their cry because of their taskmasters. I know their sufferings, and I have come down to deliver them out of the hand of the Egyptians and to bring them up

out of that land to a good and broad land, a land flowing with milk and honey, to the place of the Canaanites, the Hittites, the Amorites, the Perizzites, the Hivites, and the Jebusites. And now, behold, the cry of the people of Israel has come to me, and I have also seen the oppression with which the Egyptians oppress them."

—Exodus 3:7–9

By purpose, we must understand that God had told Abram long ago that he and his offspring would go into a strange land and that God would deliver them.

Then the LORD said to Abram, "Know for certain that your offspring will be sojourners in a land that is not theirs and will be servants there, and they will be afflicted for four hundred years. But I will bring judgment on the nation that they serve, and afterward they shall come out with great possessions. As for yourself, you shall go to your fathers in peace; you shall be buried in a good old age.

And they shall come back here in the fourth generation, for the iniquity of the Amorites is not yet complete."

—Genesis 15:13–16

God is the constant in life, and we must keep him before our eyes. Let us all resolve and firmly commit to the mantra that God is first, and I am second. His will first then my will, but only if my will harmonizes with His. God was fulfilling his work in the deliverance of Israel.

God Called Moses to Accomplish His Work

Moses didn't go out to the desert to become the leader of God's people; he went out to feed his sheep. While feeding the sheep, he saw a bush burning but not consumed, and he heard a voice speak to him, saying, among other things, "Come, I will send you to Pharaoh that you may bring my people, the children of Israel, out of Egypt" (Exod. 3:10). The breakdown looks like this:

1. I = God
2. Will send thee = Moses
3. To = Pharaoh
4. That you (Moses) may bring my (God's) people (Israel) out of Egypt.

Our focus should narrow in on God; note the independence of God. He has decided to deliver his people. He heard their cry, he was moved by their groaning and suffering, and he has come down to deliver them. Everyone else is to fall in line with God's desires. Moses is to obey and go down to Egypt. When he arrives and delivers the message, Pharaoh is to obey and submit to God's instructions and let his people go. Upon being released by the obedience of Pharaoh, Israel is to follow Moses out of Egypt and go serve God at the mount. God's will, will be done.

The Sovereign Will of God Is What Is to Be Done

When we read the account of the Hebrew exodus from Egypt, however, the plan does not go well at first. Moses is resistant to God's commands; he asks many questions. He makes excuses for why he shouldn't be chosen to go. He says he's not the one God should choose; he doesn't even know God's name, and they wouldn't believe him if he did go. When all of his excuses failed, Moses simply said, "I can't speak well; get someone else." It takes God a while and some convincing to get the leader to even agree to go (Exod. 3:11–4:16).

When Moses finally agrees to go, he is met with resistance by Pharaoh. Moses delivers God's message, but Pharaoh surprises Moses (not God) with his refusal:

> Afterward Moses and Aaron went and said to Pharaoh, "Thus says the LORD, the God of Israel, 'Let my people go, that they may hold a feast to me in the wilderness.'" But Pharaoh said, "Who is the LORD, that I should obey his voice and let Israel go? I do not know the LORD, and moreover, I will not let Israel go."

> —Exodus 5:1–2

Israel was excited to hear the news of deliverance but was quickly disappointed when Pharaoh refused. Instead of releasing them, he made their work harder by taking the straw and demanding the same output. After this, their joy was turned to sorrow, and they were upset with Moses.

Of course, we know that in the end, God's will was done. Moses went to Egypt; Pharaoh let God's people go; and Israel followed Moses out of Egypt to the mountain of God to worship.

The Basis of Leadership Is God's Purpose and Design
Those who follow must understand that the leader is doing what God purposed, not what he, the leader, has decided. As you read the verse that follow make this connection. When God appoints a position that person (s) represent God. Note how Scripture connects God directly to the leader. To follow the leader God appoints, is to follow God, it is not about the leader it is all about God's design and will.

Moses and Israel
Israel began to believe that Moses was just a man leading them. At times, they thought he was doing a bad job, and they turned against him. On several occasions, Moses and God confronted Israel with an

appeal for understanding that refusal to follow God's leader is refusal to follow God.

> They set out from Elim, and all the congregation of the people of Israel came to the wilderness of Sin, which is between Elim and Sinai, on the fifteenth day of the second month after they had departed from the land of Egypt. And the whole congregation of the people of Israel grumbled against Moses and Aaron in the wilderness, and the people of Israel said to them, "Would that we had died by the hand of the LORD in the land of Egypt, when we sat by the meat pots and ate bread to the full, for you have brought us out into this wilderness to kill this whole assembly with hunger..." So Moses and Aaron said to all the people of Israel, "At evening you shall know that it was the LORD who brought you out of the land of Egypt, and in the morning you shall see the glory of the LORD, because he has heard your grumbling against the LORD. For what are we, that you grumble against us?" And Moses said, "When the LORD gives you in the evening meat to eat and in the morning bread to the full, because the LORD has heard your grumbling that you grumble against him—what are we? Your grumbling is not against us but against the LORD." Then Moses said to Aaron, "Say to the whole congregation of the people of Israel, 'Come near before the LORD, for he has heard your grumbling.'"

—Exodus 16:1–9

To murmur and complain against Moses was to murmur and complain against God. Israel was to obey Moses because God had commanded Moses to lead its people. This premise is constant with any role that God has designed and appointed leaders to. Miriam and

Aaron in Numbers 12 and Korah, Dathan, and Abiriam in Numbers 16, each learned this lesson the hard way. Those who follow must obey God's Word and submit to those God has appointed to lead.

Government to Citizens

> Let every person be subject to the governing authorities. For there is no authority except from God, and those that exist have been instituted by God. Therefore whoever resists the authorities resists what God has appointed, and those who resist will incur judgment. For rulers are not a terror to good conduct, but to bad. Would you have no fear of the one who is in authority? Then do what is good, and you will receive his approval, for he is God's servant for your good. But if you do wrong, be afraid, for he does not bear the sword in vain. For he is the servant of God, an avenger who carries out God's wrath on the wrongdoer. Therefore one must be in subjection, not only to avoid God's wrath but also for the sake of conscience. For because of this you also pay taxes, for the authorities are ministers of God, attending to this very thing. Pay to all what is owed to them: taxes to whom taxes are owed, revenue to whom revenue is owed, respect to whom respect is owed, honor to whom honor is owed.

> —Romans 13:1–7

Citizens toward Government

These verses from Paul instruct those in Christ how to live as citizens. Consider these points that stand out in the verses above. Citizens are to be subject to government. If they resist the ordinance they resist God. Citizens are to do that which is good, because those who rule are ministers of God. Citizens are to live lawful lives and follow the ordinances. This means being subject to the government's authority and paying taxes. Citizens are to give due respect to those who govern, pay debts and live like they reflect God on the earth.

Peter Makes the Same Point as Paul

Be subject for the Lord's sake to every human institution, whether it be to the emperor as supreme, or to governors as sent by him to punish those who do evil and to praise those who do good. For this is the will of God, that by doing good you should put to silence the ignorance of foolish people. Live as people who are free, not using your freedom as a cover-up for evil, but living as servants of God. Honor everyone. Love the brotherhood. Fear God. Honor the emperor.

—1 Peter 2:13–17

Members to Elders

Obey your leaders and submit to them, for they are keeping watch over your souls, as those who will have to give an account. Let them do this with joy and not with groaning, for that would be of no advantage to you.

—Hebrews 13:17

Wives to Husbands

The husband should give to his wife her conjugal rights, and likewise the wife to her husband. For the wife does not have authority over her own body, but the husband does. Likewise the husband does not have authority over his own body, but the wife does. Do not deprive one another, except perhaps by agreement for a limited time, that you may devote yourselves to prayer; but then come together again, so that Satan may not tempt you because of your lack of self-control.

—1 Corinthians 7:3–5

Wives, submit to your own husbands, as to the Lord.

—Ephesians 5:22

Now as the church submits to Christ, so also wives should submit in everything to their husbands.

—Ephesians 5:24

However, let each one of you love his wife as himself, and let the wife see that she respects her husband.

—Ephesians 5:33

Wives, submit to your husbands, as is fitting in the Lord.

—Colossians 3:18

Older women likewise are to be reverent in behavior, not slanderers or slaves to much wine. They are to teach what is good, and so train the young women to love their husbands and children, to be self-controlled, pure, working at home, kind, and submissive to their own husbands, that the Word of God may not be reviled and so train the young women to love their husbands and children.

—Titus 2:3–5

Likewise, wives, be subject to your own husbands, so that even if some do not obey the word, they may be won without a word by the conduct of their wives, when they see your respectful and pure conduct. Do not let your adorning be external—the braiding of hair and the putting on of gold jewelry, or the clothing you wear—but let your adorning be the hidden person of the heart with the imperishable beauty of a gentle and quiet spirit, which in God's sight is very precious. For this is how the holy women who hoped in God used to adorn themselves, by submitting to their own husbands, as Sarah obeyed Abraham, calling him lord. And you are her children, if you do good and do not fear anything that is frightening.

—1 Peter 3:1–6

From the above God's expectations of wives is clear. The passages teach that wives are to render due benevolence to their husbands. A wife is to be faithful to God and this moves her to submit herself to her husband. Her relationship with God instructs her to reverence her husband. She does so because she is a spiritual person who lives a spiritual life. Because God directs her life she is self-controlled and pure of heart. She works at home and is kind. These are God's word to his daughter.

As the instructions continue God expects to shape her character into his. She is sober minded, meek and fueled by a godly character. She even sees her non-believing husband as potentially being won by the conduct of her godly life. This is the case for a woman professing belief in and a relationship with God and Christ. This is evidenced by the reason that is given. This godly woman's life is lived so that the Word of God may not be reviled. It is a difficult thing for the cause of Christ, when those professing him refuse to live their profession.

God Designed All of These Roles

- God established the home (Gen. 2:18–25).
- God established government (Gen. 9:6; Rom. 13:1–9).
- God established Moses's leadership of Israel (Exod. 3:10).
- God established elders leading the flock (Acts 20:28).
- God established husbands leading their wives (1 Cor. 11:3, 8–9).

Those who are led must see themselves as following God's design and not fixate on the human instruments God uses. God's Word is the basis of judgment and blessing. In order to please him, we must submit ourselves to him. Neither the leader nor the follower can disobey God because of the actions or inactions of the other. As a wife I must do what God told me to do, even if my husband won't.

15

MY HUSBAND WON'T LEAD—
WHAT CAN I DO?

Many wives have asked God, leaders, and themselves, "What if my husband doesn't lead or doesn't do what he is supposed to do?" When I wrote earlier about wives not following, I said that some might admit to not following but will explain their actions due to something lacking on their husband's part. It is only reasonable to think there might be some men who are thinking the same thing.

Some husbands may admit that they are not leading as God would have him to, but then argue that there is good reason for it. Though he should know there is no justifiable reason for disobeying God. The reasons he offers, may be the same as many of those offered by a wife in such a circumstance. To him these reasons could explain why she can conclude that he is not leading. First let's discuss why he may not be leading. Second let's discuss what she can't do even if he is not leading. Finally let's discuss what she can do if he is not leading. First, let us notice some reasons he may not be leading.

He May Disagree About His Duty To Lead

He could agree with radical feminism. It might seem surprising, but it really is not at all. Our culture does an amazing job convincing us that God is wrong. So a husband may disagree with God that a man should lead a woman. He might believe there is no distinction in the roles of husband and wife. So despite what scripture says, he will have no leader in his home, only partners. He is defiant and believes that God is wrong on this one. Or in his mind, he thinks leading his wife is not very nice. Since he is nicer than God he would never see himself as "leading" his wife, so he doesn't.

He May Be Misinformed

Not everyone who ends in the previous place does so with evil intention. This man might believe what he has been taught about men and himself—namely, that men are incapable, thickheaded oafs who can't do anything right. It could be that he has never seen a male lead, and he doesn't believe he can or should. He watched his mother lead his father, so he thought his wife should lead him. If he was ignorant, after reading this book, he should be ignorant no more.

He Asked His Wife To Lead

We will all appear before God one day to answer for the things done in this life (2 Cor. 5:10). How the man who took what God gave him and, without God's approval, gave it to his wife will answer, I am not sure. How the woman who accepted it, knowing that God didn't give it to her, will answer, I am not sure. Still, some husbands believe it is a good idea to abdicate the role God gave them and give it to their wives. Therefore, they are not leading because they asked her to lead.

The Most Popular Reason Is "She Won't Follow!"

Like her, if he is giving this reason, it is likely not reached lightly and without much thought. These men know that God instructs them to lead. And there are those who have tried, at least in their minds, to do what God desires and to be good husbands. These men find themselves in an impossible situation in their minds. They know that what they are about to do is contrary to their vows and God's design, and yet they feel compelled to do it anyway. Some reasons could include the following.

Financial Mismanagement

Some women have wasted more money than a rapper or ballplayer in the 1980s. The house finances look like a sieve. Money comes in, but it goes out quicker. Some husbands may have pled and pled, but their wives must keep up appearances for everyone else. Their friends have name-brand purses; they must have them too.

A wife has a five-hundred-dollar purse on her arm and can't buy a taco for lunch. Her husband has prayed to God for this woman to change, but she hasn't. He has cried a river of tears and sought ways to make more money. He has felt the bitter disappointment and endured the biting remarks regarding his failure to provide. And now he has given up. He may argue that he is not leading, but in his mind there is good reason for it.

Immoral Sexual Behavior

Men aren't the only ones who are unfaithful. Some wives have cheated on their husbands. The husband suspected, and it was finally confirmed. Some have endured this multiple times. He endured the lies, the shame, the hurt, the betrayal, and the total loss of trust. Or maybe she is just a chronic flirt. He watches as she constantly flirts with, touches, compliments, and compares him to other men. Sometimes it may even happen at worship, and he stands there and puts on a happy face.

Poor Followship Skills

Surely if you can have poor leaders, you can have poor followers. And in his estimation, he is not leading because she is a poor follower. She does not manage herself or her time well. Her chief aim in life is managing him. She does not keep her word but demands that he keep his. She starts things and stops them almost as quickly. She is not supportive of him in any way. He has plans, but she never gets behind them.

She is so hypocritical in her judgment of him while constantly excusing herself for the same things, but according to her, it is never the same thing. He concludes that she won't listen, so she can do it herself. He has checked out and is no longer leading.

These are some of the reasons he might set forth to explain why he is not leading. Like him, every one of these reasons might be disputed or modified by his wife. The point is that, for whatever reason, he is not leading, so what can she do? In answering the question, let's first examine some things she can't or shouldn't do. By "can't," I mean she can't take these actions with God's approval; by "shouldn't," I mean she can, but doing so will hurt not help her marriage.

What a Woman Must Not Do If Her Husband Isn't Leading

Withdraw and Turn Inward

You must not lose yourself on account of his action or inaction. It may not feel like a choice, but you must not dwell on the negative. It is more helpful to consider and accentuate the positive. You will be troubled if you maximize your burdens and minimizes God's blessings. God established this role; it does work. If you are in Christ you have joy and there is always something to be thankful for.

You Must Not Become Contentious

What makes any of us believe that saying it louder will cause people to understand us and believe us? Proverbs 14:1 teaches, "Every wise woman buildeth her house: but the foolish plucketh it down with her hands." You might dispute the cause and effect of his not leading, and you could be right. But being a contentious wife is not the solution to any problem. Rarely does insulting someone result in a better outcome to a present problem. How do you respond to people's complaints after they insult you?

You Must Not Return Evil for Evil

This will be tempting and easy, but it will not be right. If you are a good follower, don't ruin it with sin. No matter the cause, it is never right to do wrong. Romans 12:17 says, "Repay no one evil for evil, but give thought to do what is honorable in the sight of all." Your example, like his, is that Christ our Lord never returned evil for evil, and neither should you.

You Must Not Tell The World How Bad He Is

A man's wife is his press agent; you will largely spin the narrative that others will believe about him. A good question, then, is what story are others reading about your husband from you? Some people may think a man to be a pretty good guy, but when they hear his wife talk about him, they will learn that he is actually not worth the heat caused by rubbing two nickels together.

Some women may say, "I'm not pretending for him," and so she tells everyone who will listen all of their business. Ladies, it is not pretending; it is protection (see Matthew 7:12). Let me suggest this: if you are the only one in the group running down your husband, you ought to be quiet and ask yourself why. The other women surely have problems, but they aren't running down their husbands.

They might know what you don't, that whatever they are going through will pass. They will overcome this problem as they have others. Or they may know they would not want their husbands running them down to his friends and family. You and your husband will make up, forget, and move on. But, those who read your narrative of him never will. Especially if they are your family, family members will always remember what you told them about your husband.

You Must Not Take Over and Become the Leader

His lack of leadership does not permit you to lead; this is the simple truth that everyone must come to agree with. We already understand it and practice it in other realms of leadership. Poor leadership from elders does not confer leadership to the members. Poor parenting does not transfer leadership to children. The people in those roles are the problem, not the arrangement. Any time we go against God's design, we sin; it doesn't matter what anyone else has or has not done. God's question to Adam was, "Did you eat of the tree?" His ultimate answer was, "I did eat." God will ask every wife, "Did you remain in your role?" Her answer cannot be, "Well, he got out of his, so I got out of mine." Adam shows us that this kind of explanation fails with God.

You Must Not Turn Away from God

Maybe you have seen the triangle with the husband and wife at the bottom and God at the top. It is a major oversight that people make when considering the triangle that when the man and woman break the connection with each other, they also break the connection with God. A wife who is challenged by her husband must not conclude that God is the problem. Poor or no leadership is not God's design. The role is designed by God; the position is occupied by men. The people filling those roles will work best if they live according to God's instructions.

If the designer of a device gives instructions on the use of the product, and the user does not follow the instructions, we don't fault the designer. In every instance where leadership occurs, there are examples of it being done poorly or not at all, and there are examples of it being done well and correctly. Turning against or away from God is never the solution to any problem we encounter. Following God is not the problem in anyone's marriage; refusing to follow God will pose a problem in everyone's marriage.

You Must Not Close Your Spirit

I have heard it said that women are like plants; they need water and warmth. The water is the nutrition from which she grows, and the warmth is affection through which she will open up and blossom. Without either of these, her soil or spirit will become brittle; she will wilt close her spirt and slowly die.

When a woman is not loved and treated with honor, she will tell her husband, but he might not know what is happening. She may not even know it, but her drive, desire, and willingness to fight become less and less. His rejection and disregard of her concerns and feelings hurt her deeply. And like a plant that has no water or sunshine, her spirit dries up.

She knows that she deserves better; she knows she needs and deserves his warmth and affection, but she is not getting them. If she knows her Bible, she also knows that the Lord stated her worth: "For what is a man profited, if he shall gain the whole world, and lose his own soul? or what shall a man give in exchange for his soul?" (Matt. 16:26). The Lord's point is that one soul is worth the entire creation.

Her worth is more than the whole world, and she feels like she is being treated like a discarded piece of gum. Still, her husband may one day come around. He may hear God's Word because God alone has the power to change us. And he may sincerely apologize for all of the things he has done and for the way he has treated her.

She may one day get the very thing she has always wanted from him, but it might be too late. Because of the drought of care and affection, she has closed her spirit toward him. For many women this can be the greatest threat to their marriage and faith. She may not know it now but her biggest enemy might be herself. Will she open her spirit again once she has closed it? Will she be in a place where she can accept his apologies? Every wife must guard against closing her spirit to her husband. Start with this truth, God never closed his toward you.

If you're spirit is closed you should do what anyone in a dark cavernous place would do. Look for the light and follow it out. Christ is the light, follow him. Follow the sinless lamb of God out of the darkness and once again bask in his light. Chances are good that you and God might also be in a dark place. A good indication of your relationship with spouse is your relationship with God. The final section of this book deals with love and forgiveness. To get out of the darkness you will need a good helping of both. You can because you are God's daughter. Better to not close your spirit than to work to reopen it.

You Must Not Have Unbiblical Expectations

One of the great disappointments in marriage is unmet expectations. Shedding the world's mantras of radical feminism, a wife might ask herself a few questions like, " what do I want from him, and why do I want it?" She might also inquire about what she expected from marriage when she entered marriage, see chapter 2? The truth is that we can all come into marriage with the wrong thinking, thus expecting the wrong things the result is disappointment.

This is a very important question to consider: are your expectations the same as God's requirements? A husband could have met God's requirements and failed to meet his wife's expectations. God requires a man to provide for his household (1 Tim. 5:8). Providing shelter is not the same as a particular kind of shelter. We are to have food and clothing and be content (1 Tim. 6:6–9). Meeting the expectations about which types of food, how often we eat out, and what names are on the clothing are different matters.

Like you're husband, you must remember that your primary relationship is with God. Your husband is to lead, but you are ultimately responsible for your own relationship with God. None of us will convince God that any wrong we have done becomes right because someone did us wrong first. We will all stand before Christ and give an answer to him for our behavior. And what will we say to him about why we returned evil for evil?

What Can A Woman Do?

Hebrews 10:28–39 speaks of enduring hardship in view of the reward that is to come. If the subject of this book were easy, it wouldn't be marriage. Dealing with mistreatment in a marriage is difficult because no one can make you feel better or worse than your spouse. There are tons of women looking for answers in the Bible to deal with the pain of mistreatment in their marriages. But while the world will tell you to leave, don't cleave, God would tell you to follow the example of Jesus. Here are some biblical answers to the question, "What can I do if my husband won't lead?"

You Can Pray To God

Pray to your God, the one you love with all of you're heart, soul, mind, and strength. Pray first for yourself, Jesus did. The Lord prayed for himself; it is recorded in John 17. Pray for your spirit, attitude and actions. Prayer for you're husband. You stood before God and witnesses and vowed your love and devotion to this man for better or worse. If you are receiving worse, you vowed to love him through it, so pray for strength to keep your vow. Pray for his heart and pray for his soul. If he is doing wrong, your husband is at odds with God, and he needs prayer; he could lose his soul. Those who oppose God fail.

Pray for your family and their future. If either of you come from divorced families, you know how devastating divorce is. If the train your marriage is on continues on the course it is on, it may end at the depot of divorce. It is easy to believe in prayer when we don't need it. When crisis of this nature hits the life of a Christian, prayer is the weapon of choice.

According to scripture, prayer is designed to provide comfort, give strength, and provide motivation to continue. Prayer is also said to give peace and keep our hearts.

Do not be anxious about anything, but in everything by prayer and supplication with thanksgiving let your requests be made known to God. And the peace of God, which surpasses all understanding, will guard your hearts and your minds in Christ Jesus. Finally, brothers, whatever is true, whatever is honorable, whatever is just, whatever is pure, whatever is lovely, whatever is commendable, if there is any excellence, if there is anything worthy of praise, think about these things. What you have learned and received and heard and seen in me—practice these things, and the God of peace will be with you.

—Philippians 4:6–9

When we need prayer most, we tend to do it least. When we need to believe in it most, we tend to believe it the least. When we need to hold on to it with all of our strength, we tend to open our hands and allow it to slip through our fingers. Many a wife is certain that her trials and afflictions are due to her husband's lack of love and poor leadership, so what should she do about it?

Pray!

Our culture and social media treat prayer like a spiritual trinket. It is no more than a nice accessory to the Christian's wardrobe. It is connected to the Christian's armor. After God's soldier is outfitted for battle he prayers (Eph. 6:12-18). We wear it like a nice piece of jewelry. We talk about it and show it off to our friends, but it serves no real purpose it is just nice to have.

Jesus was about to be beaten and crucified, and he prayed (Matt. 26). After his prayer he was still beaten and crucified. The apostles were threatened with being beaten, and they prayed (Acts 4:21–34). Later they were beaten. Paul and Silas were beaten and imprisoned, and at around midnight they prayed (Acts 16:25).

If a woman's husband is refusing to lead, has given up on leading, or is a poor leader, now more than ever, she should pray. A spiritual person should do spiritual things. This is not the time to listen to carnal-minded people giving worldly advice. This is the time to be spiritual and do spiritual things. Now is the time to follow the example and teaching of Jesus.

For What Should You Pray?

When our Lord and others were in crisis, the power was not found simply in the fact that they prayed; it was also in what they prayed. Jesus prayed, "Let this cup pass from me nevertheless not my will but thy will be done (Matt. 26:39) (KJV)." The apostles prayed that God would "grant thy servant boldness to preach (Acts 4:29). (KJV)" Paul wrote of his experience in Philippians and said the things he experienced helped to further the gospel (Phil. 1:12–13). He also revealed that his actions provided an example for others to emulate (Phil. 1:14).

If a wife has faithfully followed the Lord, and her family is a mess because of the poor leadership of her husband, though time has gone by, lives have been affected, and years or maybe decades have been lost, should this woman not pray as hard and as faithfully as she ever has? This is not that three-minute breakfast prayer; this may have to be that daily, weekly, monthly, or even all-year prayer. And she should keep doing right by God and her marriage in her life. Because prayers aren't answered the way we think they should we often stop praying. But we don't just stop praying, then we start doing wrong ourselves.

You Can Examine Yourself
We all have a tender place in our hearts for women who are suffering and this is proper, but I have done enough marriage counseling to know it takes two to tango. If you are striving to live for God, you will not spin a one-sided tale of how bad he is and how perfect you are. God exhorts us all to take a self-examination to see if we are in the faith and to see if Christ is in us (2 Cor. 13:5).

Ask yourself have I done what God commanded me to do? This is not to approve or disprove any accusation made by your husband, but it will temper your actions and reactions toward him. The first relationship is with God; if you are not willing to obey God, why would you expect your husband to obey God? You may need to repent to God for your sins against him and if necessary apologize to your husband if you have sinned against him (Psalm 51:4).

This does not mean that your husband is not doing wrong; it just means you shouldn't join him in doing wrong he's doing. Each person who does wrong will be judged by God for the wrong he or she does (Col. 3:25). God's expectations of those who follow him don't end when that person is done wrong by someone else. See Jesus 1 Peter 2:21-25.

You Can Search The Scriptures
We can't live the scriptures if we don't know the scriptures. So often we don't want to change. We want the things around us to change while we remain the same. Learning God's Word will change us, and

then a new us will change the world. This would be a great time to study and learn what God says on the topic of marriage.

What does scripture say about marriage (Gen. 2:18–25)? What does the scripture say about your role in marriage (Eph. 5:22–32, 1 Pet. 3:1–6)? You need confidence in God's design and the God who designed it. The right to be loved and led reside in scripture. God needs to be your ally, and scripture needs to be your counselor (Prov. 2:6).

Follow Jesus's example in dealing with people. Read the gospel of Christ, take his yoke, and learn from him. Then walk in the steps of the Savior (1 Pet. 2:21–25). Learning the scripture will take your mind and replace it with the mind of Christ (Phil. 2:5). It is amazing how we can appeal to scripture to be treated as God teaches and then reject God's teaching when he tells us how to behave when we're being mistreated.

The beatitudes apply to every disciple of Jesus Christ (Matt. 5:3–12). The character our Lord desires us to have will be tested inside of our marriages. It seems we all think the character traits of Matthew 5:3–12 apply only to our dealing with the world. So we go out to those who reject Jesus and shine our light for Jesus. Then we come home to our marriages and turn off our lights and behave like the devil. This is not what Jesus has in mind for us. Pray for them who despitefully use you has application at home. That prayer might be for your husband.

You Can Seek Counsel

Everyone who follows has recourse when leaders don't lead. Israel had recourse to her leaders, citizens to government, members to elders, and certainly wives to husbands. God gave us a family, and he told the older sisters to teach the younger women (Titus 2:3–5). You are a wife with a husband, if he is misbehaving this is not a new thing. Since others have gone through it and hopefully come out on the other side closer to the Lord you can get help.

Schedule an appointment with the elders. You're a member and a sheep under their care. They are charged with watching for your soul. The appeal is to God and scripture, and you're husband should be yielding to the same. Elders (pastors) are there to watch for the souls of the members (Heb. 13:17). They can't do their jobs if members don't share their problems and concerns with them.

Seek professional counseling. There are times when things are beyond the skill and purview of elders and preachers. The marriage may be helped by a neutral party who is knowledgeable and skilled at counseling. Counselors should have God's wisdom as the basis of their counsel, lest God's people get counsel from those who disagree with God.

You Can Talk With Her Husband

This may seem obvious, and she may say, "Of course I told him," but that is the point. If you were hurt or angry, these talks were not talks at all. They might have started out with talking in mind but moved to accusations being made and voices escalating. After praying, learning scripture, taking a self-examination, and seeking counsel, she may be ready to talk.

One idea would be to draw word pictures or parables to help him understand how his actions make you feel. You can invite him to see his actions through your eyes. Maybe write a letter. Writing letters can allow us to express our thoughts without interruption. We can relax and think clearly with less anger or frustration. It is hard to say what you need to say in the heat of an argument.

The longer the talks go it seems the less that gets resolved. This talk can be different because it can begin with prayer. Here is a great opportunity to reconnect on something spiritual. Inviting God into the conversation will help both of you behave during the conversation. It is hard to invite God in and then behave like the devil. Try talking about seeking peace and solutions instead of about who is right or wrong. Ultimately we want to mend the relationship, right?

Include in the conversation the realization that you can both do better by God and each other then commit to trying. Try a talk that includes the Bible, and use specific verses and examples from scripture to help yourselves both do better. Share your concerns with your husband. Something he is doing or refusing to do is causing his wife pain. No one will enjoy being exposed. But if he is trying to please God, he will consider his actions in light of God's Word.

A woman's greatest allies are God and Christ. If her husband is willing to submit to God, she has great hope that he will treat her as God instructs. The head of every man is Christ (1 Cor. 11:3). If they are in Christ, they are brother and sister in the Lord (1 Pet. 3:7). She is appealing to him to accept and obey God's design. Encourage him to read your section of this book, and you read his then discuss what you learned, about God yourself and your spouse.

You Can Stay In You're Role

It will be the toughest thing to do, but it is the only thing you can do with God's approval. The only way to help you're marriage is to remain faithful to God. Peter said that a faithful wife could win her unbelieving husband by her righteous life (1 Pet. 3:1-2). This demonstrates the power of God's word to those who don't believe, how much more if you have a believing husband.

God said to submit to your husband: "Wives, submit to your own husbands, as to the Lord" (Eph. 5:22); "Now as the church submits to Christ, so also wives should submit in everything to their husbands" (Eph. 5:24); "to be self-controlled, pure, working at home, kind, and submissive to their own husbands, that the Word of God may not be reviled" (Titus 2:5); "Likewise, wives, be subject to your own husbands, so that even if some do not obey the word, they may be won without a word by the conduct of their wives" (1 Pet. 3:1).

God told you to reverence your husband: "Nevertheless let every one of you in particular so love his wife even as himself; and the wife see that she reverence her husband" (Eph. 5:33); "For after this manner in the old time the holy women also, who trusted in God, adorned themselves, being in subjection unto their own husbands: Even as Sarah obeyed Abraham, calling him lord: whose daughters ye are, as long as ye do well, and are not afraid with any amazement" (1 Pet. 3:5–6).

You must believe God, you must believe you can! We are what we believe if you don't believe you can reverence your husband you can't. Yet, David reverenced Saul: "And Saul cast the javelin; for he said, I will smite David even to the wall with it. And David avoided out of his presence twice" (1 Sam. 18:11). David's actions demonstrate that, despite how Saul had treated him, he never returned the treatment: and more continued to reverence him.

Paul behaved with reverence even though the Priest behaved contrary to God's law. Paul kept the law despite the priest's behavior in breaking the law, because God told his people not to revile their rulers, (Exod. 22:28). And so Paul showed reverence regardless of how the priest behaved:

> And Paul, earnestly beholding the council, said, Men and brethren, I have lived in all good conscience before God until this day. And the high priest Ananias commanded them that stood by him to smite him on the mouth. Then said Paul unto him, God shall smite thee, thou whited wall: for sittest thou to judge me after the law, and commandest me to be smitten contrary to the law? And they that stood by said, Revilest thou God's high priest? Then said Paul, I wist not, brethren, that he was the high priest: for it is written, Thou shalt not speak evil of the ruler of thy people.
>
> —Acts 23:1–5 (KJV)

Jesus taught and practiced the same:

> Then spake Jesus to the multitude, and to his disciples, saying, The scribes and the Pharisees sit in Moses' seat: All therefore whatsoever they bid you observe, that observe and do; but do not ye after their works: for they say, and do not. For they bind heavy burdens and grievous to be borne, and lay them on men's shoulders; but they themselves will not move them with one of their fingers. But all their works they do for to be seen of men: they make broad their phylacteries, and enlarge the borders of their garments, and love the uppermost rooms at feasts, and the chief seats in the synagogues.
>
> —Matthew 23:1–6 (KJV)

The people were to follow God despite the behavior of their rulers. Every wife can remain in her role, because God told her to do it. And God's commands to her were never contingent upon her husbands behavior.

You Can Have Hope
In Christ, there is always hope because Christ is our hope (1 Tim. 1:1). We can love each other again when we love like God. We can seek each other's highest good again. But we must admit where we are then live out of our reality and not into our past. We can get over ourselves and come down from our perches of self-righteousness when we admit our parts in the problems in our marriages.

If we are willing, we can draw a line in the sand and commit to stop wanting the past to be different. We can let go of our anger and resentment. The power is in God, who empowers us. We can approximate the years we have left and decide how we want to live them. Do I want to live with God or without God? Do I want to remain married or get divorced? Do I want to live in misery or live in joy? All of these are largely choices. Feeling pain is not the same as living in misery.

By Christ, we can overcome all of our difficulties; through Christ, we can even love our enemies. He did (Rom. 5:6–8).

Every wife must know, if you do what this chapter says you shouldn't do, that will be the reason your marriage continues to suffer. If you do this chapter tells you to do, she will be changed by God from the inside out. Her situation will not have to improve, (but likely it will) maybe more importantly she will be changed within her situation.

Christ loved his enemies; surely we can love our spouses. If we love each other, we may just start to like each other again!

16

WHAT HE MEANS WHEN HE SAYS, "YOU DON'T RESPECT ME"

O ur culture, disagrees with God concerning male leadership in the home. Male leadership in the home has largely been overturned and replaced with female leadership in homes. Men are partly to blame for this reversal because many men abused their position and did not behave like Christ toward their wives (Ephesians. 5:25–29). This doesn't justify the reversal of roles it only helps to understand it.

But not all women want to take over their homes and some are weary of the accusation. Others dispute the notion of male leadership and feel justified in leading their families. The latter is likely impossible, for there is no such thing as a leaderless home. Husbands who have tried to lead their wives and family are often frustrated with what they perceive to be a lack of praise or adoration for the effort. Wives who are listening and following are tired being associated with those wives who aren't.

A wife might be tired of trying to please what appears to be a difficult man. This wife doesn't know what he wants anymore; he never seems to be satisfied. Some husbands have tried to explain what they are seeking, and most of them probably couldn't explain it, so they defaulted to the only phrase they knew. The four dreaded words for women, "You don't respect me."

This charge is offensive to her because she has bit her tongue a thousand times. She has watched while to her, decisions were made with which she disagreed and for which she was sure there was a better way. She has never yelled at him, pointed in his face, or told him where to go. She has never told him that she wasn't going to do what he said or put him down in front of the children.

Now she believes he wants a "yes woman" and this is something she simply cannot be. What his desire sounds like to her is a woman who doesn't think, never disagrees, she never feels anything but joy—a woman with no voice or mind of her own. To her it sounds like he wants a Stephford wife, and she absolutely refuses to be a robot.

After she explains to him what she thinks he means, he is shocked and says, "That is not what I mean!" To that she replies, "Well, it sure sounds like it to me." They both look at each other, frustrated and disappointed. He is not getting what he desires and believes he is due, and she has no way of knowing let alone doing what he desires.

In light of these things, let me explain what he means. Please bear in mind women may never have heard the Bible concept of reverence.

He Means Bible *Reverence*, Not Human *Respect*
He may not know it, and you probably don't know it, but the Bible describes something called reverence that a husband is due from his wife. The word is similar to respect but it is not the same. Our society has taken reverence off the menu and replaced it with a similar product that is not as good as the original. But even in English dictionaries the differences between the words are stark; in scripture, the difference is even more profound.

Ask google to define the words respect and reverence and this is what appears.

> **Respect**—a feeling of deep admiration for someone or something elicited by their abilities, qualities, or

achievements. To admire (someone or something) deeply as a result of their abilities, qualities, or achievements.

Reverence—a feeling or attitude of deep respect tinged with awe; veneration. The outward manifestation of this feeling: to pay reverence. A gesture indicative of deep respect; an obeisance, bow, or curtsy. The state of being revered or treated with respect tinged with awe.

Pay attention to the significance of the last definition of respect, and apply these things to your husband. The first part (the feelings of deep admiration) is based on the second part. It is based on his *abilities, qualities, or achievements*. Notice that those words and that idea is absent from the definition for reverence. People are familiar with the word *respect,* but many have never studied the word *reverence.*

The truth is many women don't even know what it means, and without knowing what it means, it will be impossible to do it. This is a very sad situation for any wife because God has commanded her to reverence her husband, and she may never have heard the word or know what it means. Consider, then, what the Bible says about reverence, this is what your husband means.

Biblical Definitions and Examples
The following are some passages dealing with reverence. The questions of what reverence is, who is to be reverenced, and how reverence is shown are all answered here.

Reverence God's Sanctuary

Ye shall keep my sabbaths, and reverence my sanctuary: I am the LORD.

—Leviticus 19:30

The sanctuary was where God met and communed with his people. They were to approach him with reverence. Brown, Driver, and Briggs (hereafter BDB) define this word as follows:

1) to fear, revere, be afraid
    1a1) to fear, be afraid
    1a2) to stand in awe of, be awed

The approach to God and the regard for God's presence from his people is answered by the definition. They were to fear, revere, and stand in awe of God's sanctuary. A reverent disposition would affect the worshipers thoughts, words and deeds toward God.

Reverence God's King

> Then king David sent, and fetched him out of the house of Machir, the son of Ammiel, from Lodebar. Now when Mephibosheth, the son of Jonathan, the son of Saul, was come unto David, he fell on his face, and did reverence. And David said, Mephibosheth. And he answered, Behold thy servant! And David said unto him, Fear not: for I will surely shew thee kindness for Jonathan thy father's sake, and will restore thee all the land of Saul thy father; and thou shalt eat bread at my table continually.
>
> —2 Samuel 9:5–7

David sent for Mephibosheth the son of Jonathan, the grandson of Saul. Saul had sworn David as his enemy and had tried to kill David many times. Saul had died in battle, and now David reigned as king. When David called for Mephibosheth his behavior might be seen as being done out of fear of reprisal.

Whether it was or not, please note what he did. He came before the king, fell on his face, and did reverence. This is not something you simply feel; neither is it a sensation of admiration. It is "the outward manifestation of this feeling: to pay reverence...a gesture indicative of deep respect; an obeisance, bow, or curtsy."

Mephibosheth's actions leave no doubt as to what he is doing in the king's presence. He is giving him reverence. His may be born out of fear, which is likely realized by David, who says to him, "Fear not, for I will surely show kindness for Jonathan's sake." However, in 1 Kings 1:31, Bathsheba (David's mother) comes before David and does the same thing, though she is in no danger.

Mordecai Refused To Give Reverence

Reverence can be seen by the one due it and the one who is supposed to give it. Reverence requires action so one person could refuse to give reverence to another person. In the book of Esther Haman was promoted by the king. Because of his promotion he expected everyone to reverence him. But Mordecai being a Jew couldn't offer to Haman the reverence he believed he was due. Mordecai reserved the kind of reverence Haman sought for God.

A show down ensued because other individuals did reverence Haman. They also knew that Mordecai didn't bow before Haman the way they did. Believing that Mordecai lacked conviction they told Haman to see what Mordecai would do. The point is everyone involved knew what reverence demanded Haman expected it and Mordecai refused to give it.

> And all the king's servants, that were in the king's gate, bowed, and reverenced Haman: for the king had so commanded concerning him. But Mordecai bowed not, nor did him reverence. Then the king's servants, which were in the king's gate, said unto Mordecai, Why transgressest thou the king's commandment? Now it

came to pass, when they spake daily unto him, and he hearkened not unto them, that they told Haman, to see whether Mordecai's matters would stand: for he had told them that he was a Jew. And when Haman saw that Mordecai bowed not, nor did him reverence, then was Haman full of wrath.

- Esther 3:2-5 KJV

Haman hated Mordecai for his refusal to reverence. Because of this incident, Haman sought to destroy the Jewish nation. This is the background and setting for the events in the book of Esther. Reverence can be seen and one can refuse to give reverence.

Reverence Your Husband

Nevertheless let every one of you in particular so love his wife even as himself; and the wife see that she reverence her husband.

—Ephesians 5:33 KJV

It might seem strange when this verse is read in a modern Bible, and the word is *respect* instead of reverence. This is why we need to define words from the original language. We also need to appreciate that culture impacts our understanding of words. The word *respect* in our culture even when read in the Bible will fall short of what the word reverence means biblically.

To see the evidence of that, notice the definition of the word. According to Strong's concordance this is the Greek word phobeo the root meaning of which is to put to fear. Strong's definition of this word reverence in Ephesians 5:33 is this: to frighten, that is (passively) to be alarmed; by analogy to be in awe of, that is revere. According to God, wives are to phobeo their husbands.

195

Recently, I read these definitions to a sister. First, she was shocked, and then she said, "So you are telling me I am to be afraid of my husband!" Don't you love when a verse or definition is read, and someone says, "so you're telling me" as if you wrote the definition or passage?

Reverence can mean several things, depending on the context. Other concordances will give more definitions. The question is, which definition, best fits how a wife is to treat her husband? The definition that is most appropriate for how a wife is to treat her husband is, "to reverence, venerate, to treat with deference or reverential obedience" (Thayer e-sword).

And this concept and teaching is precisely the problem. Radical feminism has even influenced the righteous, so that godly women are offended by the definition. A biblical reverent disposition of a wife toward her husband is seen as distasteful and even offensive. Any woman caught so acting would be viewed as brainwashed, backward and uninformed. A man suggesting such a thing well, I may lack the words to describe how he would be viewed. And yet, this is precisely what Scripture teaches. Now can you see why we are having so many problems in our marriages.

Peter even applies the concept of reverence to a wife's action toward her non-believing husband.

> Likewise, ye wives, be in subjection to your own husbands; that, if any obey not the word, they also may without the word be won by the conversation of the wives; While they behold your chaste conversation coupled with fear.
>
> —1 Peter 3:1–2 KJV

This passage instructs the wife who is a believer how to behave toward her husband who is an unbeliever. Her manner of life can be a powerful tool to win his devotion to the Lord. Since the Lord governs her life, her interaction with her husband can help bring him to the Lord.

He will observe her life and thereby see God through her. Thayer (e-sword) defines the word *fear* at the end of verse two as 1) fear, dread, terror, 1a) that which strikes terror; 2) reverence for one's husband.

If Peter says that a wife is to behave this way toward a non-believing husband, how much more is a believing wife to behave this way toward a believing husband? Peter explains the character, priority and attitude a wife is to have toward her husband.

> While they behold your chaste conversation coupled with fear. Whose adorning let it not be that outward adorning of plaiting the hair, and of wearing of gold, or of putting on of apparel; But let it be the hidden man of the heart, in that which is not corruptible, even the ornament of a meek and quiet spirit, which is in the sight of God of great price. For after this manner in the old time the holy women also, who trusted in God, adorned themselves, being in subjection unto their own husbands: Even as Sara obeyed Abraham, calling him lord: whose daughters ye are, as long as ye do well, and are not afraid with any amazement.
>
> — 1Peter 3:3-6 KJV

You don't know how much the world has influenced you until you start learning and trying to live God's word. Isn't it amazing that the things God says a wife should focus on are the exact opposite of where the world says she should place her focus. According to Scripture she should focus on her inward beauty not her outward beauty. The emphasis shouldn't be on her clothes, make-up, purse, hair and shoes. Instead her focus should be on adorning her inner man her spirit, that which is incorruptible. Physical beauty fades away but a beautiful spirit never gets old.

The ornament of a meek and quiet spirit. You want to get on the wrong side of our culture just read these verses. Encourage women to focus and fixate on their inner beauty and to develop a meek and quiet or gentle spirit. For those who are interested in following God, the next phrase is of particular importance. Which is in the sight of God of great price. God is the one who approves of his daughters emphasis on their meek and gentle spirits not their loud flashy exterior. God teaches wives to reverence their husbands, the world teaches wives not to, which one do you follow?

A God approved example is offered next. A real life example of what Peter is saying. Even as Sara obeyed Abraham, stop did you read what God said. A holy woman who trusted in God adorned her spirit and obeyed her husband. Gasp, our world would go ballistic if they knew what the Bible taught.

Oh wait they do know what God teaches and it is the reason they are so opposed to it. If obeying her husband was not enough, Sara called him lord. I'm sad to say it but its true, I've heard women laugh at the suggestion and some have said out loud, "I would never call my husband lord." These were believers who were influenced by Radical Feminism, likely they just didn't know it.

I'm certainly not saying you have to call your husband lord, but all of this has to do with reverence. The verse ends by saying one can only be a daughter of Sara as long as she does well. If Sara did well and God approved of her obeying her husband and calling him lord. What does one suppose God thinks of the hearts of his daughters who would laugh at the passage or say they never would?

Another problem with our cultures notion of respect is that respect must be earned, so we ask the question.

Has He Earned Your Respect?

Remember we are applying the definitions to your husband and your marriage. The problem with respect in this context is that it is used as a synonym for reverence, but it is not the same. You cannot show reverence without respect, but you can give respect, especially in our culture, without reverence. The other problem is that respect is based on conditions that must be met. But according to

Peter, reverence is about the wife and her relationship with Christ. Read the definitions of respect again. Respect is "a feeling of deep admiration for someone or something elicited by their abilities, qualities, or achievements."

Since respect is based on abilities, qualities, or achievements, in the eyes of a wife, the husband may not be worthy of it. Add to that these two thoughts we have about respect: if you want respect you have to earn it; and if you want respect you have to give it. Under this construct, a husband enters marriage on a quest to earn his wife's respect, and who will determine if he completes his mission?

She Will Decide

In this arrangement, she is the prosecutor, jury, and judge and our world has taught her that this is proper and right. What will she use as a basis for her decision? Remember that our culture disputes that he should even be the leader. Our culture disagrees with God that each person has a role within the marriage. And by our cultural standards, he will only be worthy of respect if his abilities, qualities, or achievements warrant it.

He Must Take Care of Her

According to our world and its concept of respect, when a man becomes a husband his task begins, he must earn his wife's respect. To do so, he must take care of her emotionally. This means that he is in tune with and attentive to her emotionally. He knows her moods and is preemptive to comfort. He is not a woman, but he needs to have the emotional understanding of one. He is not a mind reader, but when she feels something, he needs to know it and know the proper response for it. After all, he is trying to earn her respect.

He also needs to know if a response is even needed, because on this day when she shares, she may just need him to be a good listener. He needs to feel what she feels when she feels it to the degree that she feels it and at whom she feels it. Lacking in this area is a major detriment to his earning her respect. Snide remarks, taking her at her word, trying to ease her pain with a joke, or failure to feel what she feels are all offenses punishable by a verdict of no respect. She keeps a mental log of his progress and depending on his actions and achievements she makes her determination.

He must also take care of her spiritually. This means he is a faithful, godly, righteous man who loves his wife as she needs to be loved. He is committed to God in a way that is surpassed only by the apostle Paul. He reads his Bible, but he is not preachy, especially toward her. He lives for God, but he does not push that she does, particularly that part about reverencing your husband.

He rarely makes mistakes, but when he does, he apologizes quickly especially if he wronged her. He loves her with a Christlike love, at least a partial Christlike love that dotes on her and coddles and cradles her but does not try to lead or rule over her. Of course, Christ does lead and rule the church. Sin in this man's life is a major disappointment; it will be judged severely. Trying to lead her and hold her to scripture is a true miscarriage of justice, and he will not be pardoned or respected.

He must also take care of her physically. This means she lives in a home of her choosing. Said home is adorned with the things she desires. He is to do all of this with a smile; because he is to take care of her emotionally.

The world will also tell her that she needs the purses she wants, the shoes she desires, the clothes she enjoys, and he must not forget the spas, the nails, and the hair because she needs to relax from all the stress in her life. He must make sure that she is secure in her life.

While some of that may seem extreme, That is a pretty good picture of the way our culture teaches women men are to behave in marriage. Most women have never questioned it, because one it is a pretty good arrangement and two they really believe it is how a husband is to behave to earn her respect. Such has been the power and influence of Radical Feminism, even in the church.

I don't have to tell you that most men have and are failing miserable trying to earn respect in this way. Men feel the weight of being failures and disappointments to their wives and wives are wondering how could what I signed up for have gone so wrong. God never taught this concept so it has no place in the relationship of marriage.

The world is right at least in this regard; to please God, he must provide for his wife emotionally, spiritually, and physically. However, our world has him doing these things to earn her respect, and thus sends them both down a road of misery and failure.

The Problem

He could take care of her emotionally, physically and spiritually but he might not meet her specifications,. And if he fails to meet her specifications, then he is not worthy of respect. But there is more to it than that: if he does some of these things well but fails at others, he's still not worthy of her respect. Suppose he does these things, but some of them dip today—he was on point emotionally, but he failed spiritually. Then he is not worthy of her respect. Because she is the prosecutor, jury, and judge, the saying becomes their reality: "happy wife; happy life," or "if Mama ain't happy, nobody's happy." Under this arrangement, rarely is mama going to be happy, and it will always be his fault. This is the sad state of many marriages.

The Bigger Problem

If he is over her—and according to God, he is—then how can *he* do all of these things to *her* specifications? Who is leading whom? If he is over her, he will necessarily have his own ideas about the direction of the family. He is not a woman, so he cannot be in tune with her emotionally as if he were. He can and should nurture her emotional health, but he is not a mind reader.

He does not have a menstrual cycle; even among those who say men have a cycle, not one of them in their right minds would dishonor women by suggesting they are the same. He will fail to meet the emotional needs described above, not because he doesn't want to but because they are impossible for him to meet. He is not holding out on her, he just doesn't think or feel the way she does about some things. Should he care, yes, should he listen yes, but he will use his mind to hear and respond to what she has expressed not hers. We are different and those differences manifest themselves in situations within marriage.

He should nurture her spiritual health. But he is her leader, and if he is a godly, righteous man, he must take the whole Bible that is applicable to marriage and use it in their lives. He must lead her. He must love her as Christ loves the church, but sometimes Christ disagreed with the actions of the church (Rev. 2–3). If he loves her the way Christ loved the church, according to the world, he will fail.

He ought to provide for her physically. She should have security in her life, but that might mean they live in a smaller house than she desires. It might mean she can have some shoes, clothes, and the rest, but it might not be what the world has convinced her she must have or what she may desire. Providing for her is what God commands; where they live, how many toys they have, and the extravagance of it all may not meet her approval, and he will fail to meet her expectations.

If he tries to live in his God-given role of necessity, he must run afoul of the worlds artificial standards. The bigger problem is this— simply by living as God commanded, according to our culture he will fail to earn his wife's respect. And because she believes what she has been taught she will feel justified in not awarding him her respect. By definition he hasn't earned it, because respect is awarded based on achievements, abilities or accomplishments.

These thoughts are not reflective of every woman but they do reflect our cultures disagreement with God's arrangement. And many women have been influenced by the culture in which they live.

But I Do Respect My Husband

The world has been so effective in getting us away from God that godly women's idea of respect boils down to what they don't do to their husbands.

1. I don't talk down to him.
2. I don't yell at him.

3. I'm not disagreeable in public.
4. I don't talk about him in front of other people.
5. I don't tell him what to do.

Because there are some women who do all of these things, the ones who don't believe they respect their husbands. But the ones who don't do these things are still often the disappointed prosecutors, juries, and judges above. He has not earned her respect, but as long as he is trying, she will not do these things to him. Because they don't do these things, these otherwise good women believe they are fulfilling their God-given roles because they respect their husbands. Of course, they are also the ones who keep hearing from their husbands about their lack of respect. Amazing!

The Biggest Problem
The world rejected God's Word, and we have adopted its ways. We have changed God's commands and replaced them with our concepts so that the best of the church is still nowhere near what God enjoins upon us. Given our present arrangement, a woman could respect her husband and never come close to doing what God said, which is reverencing her husband.

He may not know what he deserves, but based on the above, he is not even getting respect. What he deserves is so much more, even by our definitions. Before we look at scripture, let's read our definitions again. Reverence is: "1. a feeling or attitude of deep respect tinged with awe; veneration, 2. the outward manifestation of this feeling: to pay reverence, 3. a gesture indicative of deep respect; an obeisance, bow, or curtsy. 4. the state of being revered or treated with respect tinged with awe." If the words *veneration* or *awe* are strange to us, we might again ask ourselves, "How can I do it if I don't know what it means?" According to google's dictionary veneration is, *great respect; reverence,* and awe means *a feeling of reverential respect mixed with fear or wonder.*

Scripture demands reverence; our culture has men trying to earn respect. Even our dictionaries tell us how far off we are.

Bible Examples And Illustrations Of Reverence*Miriam, Aaron, Moses, and God*

Numbers chapter 12 records for us a situation between siblings. Aaron and Miriam, the older siblings of Moses, got together and spoke out against Moses. Verse 1 of the chapter tells us it was about a woman Moses married. Yet the rest of the chapter never records a word said about the marriage. It seems that was not really their problem at all. The true problem is best seen from what they actually said against Moses, as recorded in verse 2:

> And they said, Hath the LORD indeed spoken only by Moses? hath he not spoken also by us? And the LORD heard it.

The real problem was not who Moses had married but how prominent Moses was in Israel. Like others in Israel, Miriam and Aaron thought Moses's part was too big, and their part was too small. The end of verse 2 informs us that God heard their complaints. Verse 3 tells us that Moses was the meekest man on the earth.

Moses did not choose to lead Israel; God chose him. Since God designed the role, no one was to speak against it. Therefore, when they spoke against Moses, they spoke against God (Exod. 16:6–9). Hence the end of verse 2: "and the Lord heard it." Conversely, because Moses represented God, to reverence Moses was to reverence God. The interchange that follows among God, Miriam, and Aaron demonstrates this. Of Moses, God said,

> With him will I speak mouth to mouth, even apparently, and not in dark speeches; and the similitude of the LORD shall he behold: *wherefore then were ye not afraid to speak against my servant Moses?* And the anger of the LORD was kindled against them; and he departed. And the cloud departed from off the tabernacle; and, behold, Miriam became leprous, white as snow:

and Aaron looked upon Miriam, and, behold, she was
leprous.

—Numbers 12:7–9 [emphasis added]

According to BDB, the word rendered *afraid* in verse 8 is defined as
follows.

1) to fear, revere, be afraid
    1a1) to fear, be afraid
    1a2) to stand in awe of, be awed
    1a3) to fear, reverence, honour, respect

By the end of God's speech to Aaron and Miriam, she was plagued
with leprosy, Aaron was apologizing and pleading for her life, and Moses,
the very one they spoke against, was pleading to God to spare her.

An Amalekite, David, and Saul

As a young boy, David defeated Goliath and was thrust into the spot-
light in Israel. He had no idea about politics and popularity when he
did this, only faith. When he, Saul, and the army of Israel returned
victorious from battle, the women chanted that Saul had killed his
thousands but David his tens of thousands. Unknown to David at the
time, this angered Saul to the point of wanting to kill him. From this
time forward, Saul became David's enemy (1 Sam. 18:29).

The rest of Saul's life is largely committed to one goal: keeping
his friends close and David, his enemy, closer. Twice David was in
Saul's presence at his table, and twice Saul threw a javelin at David to
pin him to the wall (1 Sam. 18:11). David came to grips with the sad
reality that Saul wanted to take his life, so he fled to save himself.

Now on the run, David became public enemy number one. Saul
used all of his power as king to find David. He chased him all over the
country. He demanded allegiance from all in his kingdom; if anyone
was found to have helped or harbored David, they would be killed. One

servant of Saul killed eighty-five priests, men, women, and even babies because they were thought to have helped David (1 Sam. 22:16–19).

In the midst of all of this chaos and threats to his life, on two occasions David had opportunity to kill Saul. Once while chasing David, Saul entered into a cave for a bathroom break. He did not know that David and his men were hiding inside the cave. David's men urged him to kill Saul, but David refused (1 Sam. 24:1–9).

Another time, Saul pursued David, and David saw where Saul rested for the night. David and two of his men went to the campsite and stood over Saul while he slept. His men urged him to kill Saul; one of the men said he would do it for David. He promised to only strike Saul once so the pain felt would be minimal. Again David refused to kill Saul; neither did he allow his men to do it.

David refused to kill Saul for one reason: Saul was God's anointed. It didn't matter what Saul did to David; he never made Saul his enemy. David understood that to kill Saul would be to go against what God designed (1 Sam. 10:1–10).

What does any of this have to do with anything, great question? Here is the answer. In Saul's final battle, he was wounded, and to avoid being tortured by his enemy, he fell upon his sword. A young man came upon Saul and saw him dead. He took some of Saul's items and brought them to David. When David saw him approaching, he asked him where he was from and who he was. The young man said he was an Amalekite and that he had come from the battlefield. He informed David that Saul and Jonathan had died in battle. He then told David that he had happened upon Saul and that Saul was wounded. He said that Saul asked him to fall upon him and take his life. The young man said he honored Saul's request and killed him to put him out of his misery.

This young man assumed that David would be happy to hear of Saul's death for a few reasons. Saul hated David and tried to kill him; also, with Saul's death, David could now be king. For these two reasons he assumed David would reward him for his action in killing Saul. The young man greatly misjudged David on all counts and was likely very shocked to hear David's response:

And David said to the young man who told him, "Where do you come from?" And he answered, "I am the son of a sojourner, an Amalekite." David said to him, "How is it you were not afraid to put out your hand to destroy the LORD's anointed?" Then David called one of the young men and said, "Go, execute him." And he struck him down so that he died. And David said to him, "Your blood be on your head, for your own mouth has testified against you, saying, 'I have killed the LORD's anointed.'"

—2 Samuel 1:13–16

The power of David's thought must be felt and appreciated by us all. Chased, threatened, and with multiple attempts on his life, he never returned evil to Saul. Having at least two opportunities to kill Saul, he refused and prevented others from killing him. Even hearing a man suggest that he did kill him based on a request from Saul (he was lying), David had the reaction of asking the man, "How did you not fear [to fear, reverence, honor, respect] (Strong's e-sword.com) to kill the Lord's anointed?"

David's actions toward Saul provide a powerful example for every wife. God anointed Saul; therefore Saul should have been reverenced because God made him king of Israel. This brings us naturally to the next point and further illustrates the difference between modern respect and Bible reverence.

Reverence Does Not Have to Be Earned

Nevertheless let every one of you in particular so love his wife even as himself; and the wife see that she reverence her husband.

—Ephesians 5:33

The verse says something that both husband and wife are to do. Of the wife, the verse says "and the wife see that she reverence her husband." This is a command to be obeyed, not a suggestion to be vetted based on her assessment of his abilities. The wife is to reverence her husband (to reverence, venerate, to treat with deference or reverential obedience). That part of the verse is not about him; it is about her.

To appreciate this, take the other part of the verse: "Nevertheless let every one of you in particular so love his wife even as himself." Take the same approach to love that our culture takes to respect. First, love is earned; second, if you want love, you have to give love. Who will decide if a woman is worthy of love? The man will, of course. He will be the prosecutor, jury, and judge, and, based on his assessment of her abilities, achievements, and talents, he will decide if she is worthy of love. If you think telling a woman that God says she is to reverence her husband is a challenge, try telling her that she has to earn her husband's love and that he will decide if she is worthy of it.

Now why is it that no one would ever suggest that a woman has to earn her husbands love, but everyone is willing and able to easily tell a man he has to earn his wife's reverence? The verse commands the appropriate actions of both people, and the fact is it has nothing to do with the other person's behavior. It has everything to do with what God has designed and commanded, not with the recipients abilities, achievements or accomplishments.

Reverence Comes with the Office
When God designed leadership, it was God being represented. Even God as Israel's leader was not reverenced. Listen to his interchange with his people.

> A son honors his father, and a servant his master. If then I am a father, where is my honor? And if I am a master, where is my fear? says the LORD of hosts to you, O priests, who despise my name. But you say, "How have we despised your name?" By offering polluted

food upon my altar. But you say, "How have we polluted you?" By saying that the LORD's table may be
despised. When you offer blind animals in sacrifice, is
that not evil? And when you offer those that are lame
or sick, is that not evil? Present that to your governor;
will he accept you or show you favor? says the LORD
of hosts.

—Malachi 1:6–8

That a son is to honor his father is accepted, and a servant is to fear
his master. This is true simply by the dynamic of the relationship.
The confusion is, since God is both of these to Israel, why hasn't he
received the appropriate responses? Hence God's questions, "Where
is my fear and where is my honor?"

Instead of those responses, God was receiving the opposite, and
what he was receiving was inconsistent with the relationship. Instead
of honor and fear, they despised his name. Their actions disagreed
with their claims. They offered polluted food; they said the Lord's
table was contemptible; and they offered the blind in sacrifice. God's
questions are rhetorical but need to be answered. Twice he asked, "Is
this not evil?"

The clincher was when God said, "Offer that to your governor,
will he accept you or show you favor?" What a powerful, eye-opening
challenge. God tells them to take the same thing they offer to the
God of heaven and offer it to a human dignitary. He knows what
we all know—they would never have offered polluted, spoiled, rotten
food to elected officials, neither would we. If we were allowed into
their presence, we would all reverence them. If we were the chef to
prepare their food, they would eat the best we had to offer because
we reverence the position. We wouldn't have to agree with them, neither would their behavior determine the quality of food we served.

The office would drive the reverence, not the ability of the person
in office. This is God's design and the expectation of wives toward

their husbands. This is the reason the world attacks the design because design determines function. According to Genesis 2 the woman was made from the man, for the man, and was brought to the man. Therefore, she is to reverence her husband.

What Does Reverence Look Like?
In having multiple conversations with women some who want to do what God says but have never heard it. Others who do not want to do what God says because culture has influenced them. On occasion both have asked, what does reverence look like?

Consider First His Presence
Moses's presence in the congregation of Israel would not have gone unnoticed. Because he was their leader, when he was around, people would have noticed. Their actions would be consistent with those who reverenced their leader. This same dynamic would have been true of the kings of Israel when present. When Mephibosheth came before David, he bowed down and did reverence.

A generation or two ago, when a man came home, his presence had this same effect. No one bowed down, and no wife is commanded to bow before her husband today. However, when a husband came home a generation ago, he was met with reverence. He pulled his car into the driveway, and the house changed. Everyone in the house responded with joy and anticipation or with reverent fear of the one coming across the threshold, Dad was home.

His wife—the children's mom—led the charge. She met her husband and greeted him at the door. The greeting was warm and pleasant. The house was to his specifications because he had made his wishes known, and Mom led the charge in making sure they were carried out. Upon arrival, he was often given reports of the behaviors and events of the day.

For many people, this picture is not simply disagreeable; it is disgusting. "Who does he think he is?" or "You wish I would do something like that." He is not worthy of such a reaction at his arrival."

Your initial feeling when you read it will give you some insight how you view your husband. It will also help you to know if God or culture is influencing you. Maybe your view of reverence is impacting the state of your marriage.

What does his presence look like today? Now, a man comes home, and it makes no difference to anyone inside the house. Not only is there often a general disinterest at his arrival, but he is often met with, at least in his mind, animosity or displeasure at his presence. He is not met and greeted by children because, in this, Mom often leads the way as well.

He can't put his finger on it, but he knows something is wrong with this picture. He may have tried all day to provide for everyone in the house, and though he wanted to quit a thousand times, he did not. But because he didn't meet his wife's expectations, he is not worthy of respect because he hasn't earned it.

However, now he is not looking for respect; he is shooting for reverence. He knows his presence in his house should evoke a different response; what he can't believe is that no one else seems to know it. He wants to say, "A son honors his father, and a wife reverences her husband. If I am a father, where is my honor? If I am a husband, where is my reverence?"

Consider Next His Speech

When one is reverenced, what are their words heard like? Consider again how Moses was heard:

> He that despised Moses' law died without mercy under two or three witnesses: Of how much sorer punishment, suppose ye, shall he be thought worthy, who hath trodden under foot the Son of God, and hath counted the blood of the covenant, wherewith he was sanctified, an unholy thing, and hath done despite unto the Spirit of grace? For we know him that hath said, Vengeance belongeth unto me, I will recompense, saith the Lord.

> And again, The Lord shall judge his people. It is a fearful thing to fall into the hands of the living God.
>
> —Hebrews 10:28–31

Why isn't anyone afraid to fall into the hands of the living God? Who told us it was alright to reject God's word concerning reverence? Why aren't preachers afraid to tell wives that reverencing your husband is old outdated teaching that has no bearing on today? Moses words were to be reverenced by those he led. Why aren't a husbands words to be reverenced by those he leads, since God established the leadership. And since God will hold the husband responsible for what happens to those he leads.

A generation or two ago, when a husband who was met by his wife and children spoke, he was met with attention followed by obedience. Again, the one leading the cause of reverence was his wife. She championed the cause of her husband and relayed that cause to their children. She listened to what he said and followed the decisions he made, even it meant she had to change something. He shared what he liked, and that was on the menu. She was not the leader of the family; neither did she seek to be.

What does that look like today? The husband whose presence is met with indifference is likely to have his words met with indifference. His words carry little weight with his wife and children. Many a husband has conceded and thrown in the towel on leading their families. His words are now more likely repeating her words, so instead of being supported, he is now supporting his wife. Her words and presence are reverenced not his, like the other children he even jumps to when mom says. But he is still trying to earn her respect.

He needs reverence, and he should know that God thinks so as well. The Holy Spirit told Paul to write, "And ye wives *see that you* reverence your husband." She should consider that she is doing this for Jesus. God designed the dynamic and enables her to live in it. He would not require of her that which she could not do. Her husband no more needs to earn her reverence than she needs to earn his love.

No husband should base his actions on the actions of his wife and no wife should base her actions on those of her husband. Each of us must understand our personal responsibility to God. Every husband will have to answer to God for whether or not he loved his wife as God commanded him. And every wife will have to answer to God for whether or not she reverenced her husband as God commanded her.

Do I reverence my husband is not a question about men or for men. Do I reverence my husband is a question that every wife must answer, if you are a wife reverence is commanded to you and the answer can only come from you.

Do you reverence your husband?

SECTION 4

Chapters 17-20

God's Word for Happy Marriages

For Us

17

WHAT IS LOVE?

Our world is big on love; it might be fair to say that we love-love. We talk about it all the time; we want to feel it when we don't. We profess it to each other when we do. When we are out of it, we want to be in it. And when we are in it, we want to make it better and have more of it. We even love things like football, Angry Birds, selfies, pizza, and our phones. We give love and we receive it. We work hard at doing it better. We even want to learn to love ourselves more. The late Whitney Houston told us that learning to love yourself is the greatest love of all.

It's been said that the greatest thing in the world is "to love and to be loved," and with this our songwriters and singers agree. I heard a line in a song many years ago that stuck with me. The man was begging his girlfriend to stay with him, and in the song he said, "If you'd stay, I'd subtract twenty years from my life." Wow!

I wasn't yet twenty at the time, so I heard a man say he loved his girlfriend so much that if she stayed, he would give his whole life for her. What an amazing commitment. We are truly head-over-heels for love. We write love letters and watch romantic movies. We celebrate Valentine's Day—a whole day dedicated to love...or a day when we help boost the bottom line of flower shops, candy makers, card companies, balloon companies, the dollar store, and jewelry companies. Either way it is probably about love.

Love is for everybody—husbands and wives, parents and children, grandparents and friends. Scripture even enjoins upon us to love our enemies. Truly, love is for everybody. Even those who are down on love are so because they tried it and it failed. This is why it seems fair to say that we love "love" but we are not alone.

God is a huge proponent of love: we could equally say heaven loves "love". How big is love in heaven? Just listen:

> Beloved, let us love one another, for love is from God, and whoever loves has been born of God and knows God. Anyone who does not love does not know God, because God is love.

> —1 John 4:7–8

In these verses, Love is exhorted—let us love one another. Love has an origin—love is from God. Love connects us to God—whoever loves has been born of God and knows God. To not love is to lack knowledge—anyone who does not love does not know God. Scripture's definition of God—God is love!

The Bible is full of love; arguably the most well-known scripture in the Bible (John 3:16) is about love. Every kind of love imaginable is spoken of in the Bible. God's love for the world is the centerpiece of the Bible.

- God's love—John 3:16.
- Friendship love—1 Samuel 20:17
- Love of enemies—Mathew 5:43–48
- Man and woman—Genesis 29:20
- An entire book in the Bible (Song of Solomon) dedicated to love.
- God loved his people—Malachi 1:2
- Christ loves the church—Ephesians 5:25

We love love heaven loves love; God loves love; and God is love. With so much attention and desire given to love in heaven and on earth, what could possibly go wrong? We all want to give and receive it, but does anyone actually know what it is?

What Is Love?

Give it a try—describe love. It is not as easy as it seems. Some possible answers could be that love is a feeling— many people describe love in terms of how they feel. I feel so good when I'm with him or her. It just feels right when we're together. Others describe love as an action. He or she does whatever I ask or I will give her the moon. This dynamic is the breakdown in many marriages. "You don't love me," she says. He retorts, "I do love you. I go to work, I pay the bills, I take out the trash, etc. If I didn't love you, I wouldn't do anything for you. She sees and knows all he does and still she says she doesn't feel loved. He might respond, "Love is something you do. It doesn't need my feelings. I show my love." Which one is right? Are they both right? The question is this, "husband, do you love your wife and wife, do you love your husband?"

What Does the Bible Say about Love?

The following material is taken from e-sword.com. The word *love* appears in scripture 311 times, in 281 verses.

The word *love* in the following verses is *Strong's* number 157: "a primitive root; to have affection for (sexually or otherwise)." As we often say in Bible study, context determines the meaning. This word is used in numerous settings, and the Bible determines what it means in a particular verse. Notice the varied contexts in which the word love is used.

Abraham Loves His Son

And he said, Take now thy son, thine only son Isaac, whom thou lovest, and get thee into the land of Moriah;

and offer him there for a burnt offering upon one of the mountains which I will tell thee of.

—Genesis 22:2 KJV

Isaac to Bless Esau (Isaac Loves a Meal)

And make me savoury meat, such as I love, and bring it to me, that I may eat; that my soul may bless thee before I die.

—Genesis 27:4 KJV

Isaac and Rebekah (A Husband Loves His Wife)

And Isaac brought her into his mother Sarah's tent, and took Rebekah, and she became his wife; and he loved her: and Isaac was comforted after his mother's death."

—Genesis 24:67

Jacob and Rachel (A Man Loves His Future Wife)

And Jacob loved Rachel; and said, I will serve thee seven years for Rachel thy younger daughter.

—Genesis 29:18

Leah and Jacob (A Wife Wants to Be Loved by Her Husband)

And Leah conceived, and bare a son, and she called his name Reuben: for she said, Surely the LORD hath looked upon my affliction; now therefore my husband will love me.

—Genesis 29:32

A Man Desires a Woman

And Dinah the daughter of Leah, which she bare unto Jacob, went out to see the daughters of the land. And when Shechem the son of Hamor the Hivite, prince of the country, saw her, he took her, and lay with her, and defiled her. And his soul clave unto Dinah the daughter of Jacob, and he loved the damsel, and spake kindly unto the damsel.

—Genesis 34:1–3 KJV

Man's Love for God

And shewing mercy unto thousands of them that love me, and keep my commandments.

—Exodus 20:6 KJV

A Servant and a Master

If his master have given him a wife, and she have born him sons or daughters; the wife and her children shall be her master's, and he shall go out by himself. And if the servant shall plainly say, I love my master, my wife, and my children; I will not go out free.

—Exodus 21:4–5

In light of the contexts in which the word is used it can mean a wide variety of things from human love for another, including family and sexual; human appetites for objects such as food, drink, sleep or wisdom; and love for humans or God.

Another definition of *love* is *Strong's (e-sword.com)* number 160, and it is defined by BDB in the following manner:

1) love
      1a) human love for human object
            1a1)   of man toward man
            1a2)   of man toward himself
            1a3)   between man and woman
            1a4)   sexual desire
2) God's love to His people

Genesis 29:16–32 tells of the relationships of Jacob, Leah, and Rachel. Within the passages, both words are used at different times to express what people are feeling and doing toward each other.

      29:18—Jacob loved Rachel (H157)
      29:20—Jacob served for the love he had for her (H160)
      29:30—He loved Rachel (H157)
      29:32—For now my husband will love me (H157)

Just reading the passages and depending on the context, love is both a feeling and an action. One has affection for something or someone, and that moves one to act toward or on behalf of the person. These two words are the most frequently used in the Old Testament, but they are not the only words that are used.

Love in the New Testament

It does not take long to get to the concept of *love* in the New Testament. Our Lord uses the word in his first public address to man. That word is *Strong's* number G25.

Thayer Definition:

1) of persons
   1a) to welcome, to entertain, to be fond of, to love dearly
2) of things
   2a) to be well pleased, to be contented at or with a thing

Love Your Enemies

> You have heard that it was said, "You shall love your neighbor and hate your enemy." But I say to you, Love your enemies and pray for those who persecute you.

—Matthew 5:43–44 (*Strong's* G25)

The Lord is not saying one should feel good about one's enemy who hates him. This word means one does what is in the highest good of another human being, even if that human being hates you. This is what God did for us when he sent Christ to die for us when we were God's enemies (Romans 5:6-8).

Another good example of this teaching is seen in the Lord's parable often called The Parable of the Good Samaritan. The parable is recoded in Luke 10:25-37. Despite the fact that the Jews and the Samaritans hated each other, the Lord taught that a Samaritan man saw a Jewish man half dead in the street and helped him. Scripture calls this thoughtfulness and action by the Samaritan toward his enemy, love and Jesus ended his teaching by saying "go and do likewise."

Love God and Your Neighbor

> And he said to him, "You shall love the Lord your God
> with all your heart and with all your soul and with all
> your mind. This is the great and first commandment.
> And a second is like it: You shall love your neighbor as
> yourself. On these two commandments depend all the
> Law and the Prophets."

> —Matthew 22:37–40 (*Strong's* G25)

The passages say we are to love God with all of our heart. Our heart is comprised of four parts, not the muscle in our chest that pumps our blood. But rather our mind or the spirit within us. From God's perspective our heart is the center of our being we think, act and love from our heart. The four parts of our heart are our intellect, emotion, conscience and will.

To love God with all of our heart is to love him intellectually. This is the reason we must come to Jesus and learn God. Our thoughts must be directed by God's word but it is not merely intellectual. Our emotion must be stirred by what we learn. One cannot learn of Christ in the garden of Gethsemane and not be moved emotionally. We learn of our sin, we learn that Christ, the sinless Lamb of God, dies for our sins. We hear him moan, weep and wail then watch as he is beaten and crucified. If our emotions are not stirred by learning these things we can't love God with all of our heart.

But learning and feeling only take us so far. Our conscience will take the information and the feelings that are stirred and then ask us to behave in harmony with what we believe. It won't tell us what to believe it will urge or nudge us to do what we believe is right. If we do, our conscience will not hurt. It doesn't mean what we are doing is right it simply means we acted in harmony with what we thought was right.

Ideally, our consciences will be trained by God's word then we will be urged to act in harmony with what is actually right. One can have a clear conscience while doing terribly wrong things. Before he became the apostle Paul, Saul persecuted and killed Christians. After becoming a Christian he was persecuted, and when questioned he spoke of his past and his conscience. This is what he said, "And looking intently at the council, Paul said, "Brothers, I have lived my life before God in all good conscience up to this day."

-Acts 23:1

During the times he killed Christians he did what he thought was right (Acts 26:9). Clearly it wasn't right but such is the nature of our conscience. It urges us to do what we believe is right. To love God with all of your heart you must do what you believe toward God with a good conscience.

All of this then feeds to our will. Our will serves as the action center of our heart. It takes the information gleaned from the intellect but we don't always do what we know. It takes the emotion into account but we don't always do what our feelings demand. It takes the conscience into account but it can override the conscience so that we do what we believe is wrong or refuse to do what we believe is right. The will is our heart in action and it is what God and people see us do. Jesus said we could know each other by our fruit. The heart can conceal only so much, but the action (fruit) tells us what kind of tree we are (Matthew 7:15-20).

To love God with all of our heart we must do his will. Jesus frequently taught the necessity of doing to demonstrate love because love must be willed. We can't just say, think or feel we love God. We must show God we love him.

The Lord taught we must do the will of the Father (Matthew 7:21-23). Scripture teaches that Christ is the author of eternal life for all those who obey him (Hebrews 5:8-9). Jesus taught that we should not give him the the title of Lord if we refuse to obey him (Luke 6:46).

Love that does not act or is not willed into action cannot be love with all of one's heart.

John's exhortation is clear, My little children, let us not love in word, neither in tongue; but in deed and in truth (1 John 3:18). KJV

Love for God

> And many false prophets will arise and lead many astray. And because lawlessness will be increased, the love of many will grow cold.

> —Matthew 24:11–12 (*Strong's* G5368).

Thayer Definition:

1) to love
    1a) to approve of
    1b) to like
    1c) sanction
    1d) to treat affectionately or kindly, to welcome, befriend
2) to show signs of love
    2a) to kiss
    3) to be fond of doing
    3a) be wont, use to do

The Pharisees Love Places of Honor

> They do all their deeds to be seen by others. For they make their phylacteries broad and their fringes long, and they love the place of honor at feasts and the best seats in the synagogues.

> —Matthew 23:5–6

Husbands, Love Your Wives

And now the million-dollar questions: Which word is used for marriage? How is a husband to love his wife? Drum roll, please. It's *Strong's* number G25.

Thayer Definition:

1) of persons
    1a) to welcome, to entertain, to be fond of, to love dearly
2) of things
    2a) to be well pleased, to be contented at or with a thing

Husbands, Love Your Wives

> Husbands, love your wives, even as Christ also loved the church, and gave himself for it.
>
> —Ephesians 5:25

A breakdown of the passage reveals the what, who, how, and the extent of his love.

- What is he to do? Love.
- Who is he to love? His wife.
- How is he to love? As Christ also loved the church.
- Extent to which he is to love? Give himself for it.

A few verses later, more is revealed.

> So ought men to love their wives as their own bodies. He that loveth his wife loveth himself.
>
> —Ephesians 5:28 (*Strong's* G25)

- Who? Men
- What? Love
- Who? Their wives
- How? As their own bodies
- Extent? He that loveth his wife loveth himself.

The scripture states these things emphatically and follows them with evidence.

> For no man ever yet hated his own flesh; but *nourisheth and cherisheth* it, even as the Lord the church.

> —Ephesians 5:29

Nourisheth—Thayer Definition:

1) to nourish up to maturity, to nourish
2) to nurture, bring up

Cherisheth—Thayer Definition:

1) to warm, keep warm
2) to cherish with tender love, to foster with tender care

Putting the Pieces Together
The husband-wife relationship is about oneness. The picture begins to come into focus as Paul continues the analogy in Ephesians 5:30: "For we are members of his body—of his flesh and of his bones." It is helpful here to go back and read Genesis 2:21–23, because that is the place from which the point is being made:

> So the LORD God caused a deep sleep to fall upon the man, and while he slept took one of his ribs and closed up its place with flesh. And the rib that the LORD God

had taken from the man he made into a woman and brought her to the man. Then the man said, "This at last is bone of my bones and flesh of my flesh; she shall be called Woman, because she was taken out of Man."

After God made the woman and brought her to Adam, his reaction was "at last this is now bone of my bones; she is flesh of my flesh." We are the same—she is like me, she is from me, and we are one. Paul's point about the church and Christ is the same; we are members of his body. But what Paul says next takes us back to Adam and Eve:

> Because we are one, For this cause shall a man leave his father and mother, and shall be joined unto his wife, and they two shall be one flesh.
>
> —Ephesians 5:31

This is precisely what God said in Genesis:

> Therefore a man shall leave his father and his mother and hold fast to his wife, and they shall become one flesh.
>
> —Genesis 2:24

Why is he leaving and cleaving? Because she is bone of his bones and flesh of his flesh. Two have become one, and he loves her as himself.

Paul closes chapter 5 of Ephesians by drawing our attention back to Christ and his church and then gives us a final exhortation.

> This is a great mystery: but I speak concerning Christ and the church. Nevertheless let every one of you in

particular so love his wife even as himself; and the wife
see that she reverence her husband.

—Ephesians 5:32–33

What Does God's Love Look Like?

Hereby perceive we the love of God, because he laid
down his life for us: and we ought to lay down our lives
for the brethren.

—1 John 3:16

Beloved, let us love one another: for love is of God;
and every one that loveth is born of God, and knoweth
God. He that loveth not knoweth not God; for God is
love. In this was manifested the love of God toward us,
because that God sent his only begotten Son into the
world, that we might live through him. Herein is love,
not that we loved God, but that he loved us, and sent
his Son to be the propitiation for our sins.

—1 John 4:7–10

Love looks like both who God is and what God does. This is why God
can be described as *being* love. His character is love, and his behavior
comes from his character. He is what he does, and so are we. By learning about God, a husband can both be like and behave like God.

What Does This Love Do?
If God is and does anything, he gives. Long before God gave his Son
on the cross, he gave us life. Before creating us in his image, he created a world in which we could live. The world was not made in vain; it
was made to be inhabited (Isa. 45:12–18). Thought of properly, from

the opening of the Bible until the close of scripture, God is giving. The ultimate expression of his love is Jesus dying on the cross for his enemies (Rom. 5:6–8). What does love do? To ask is to answer.

Love gives—John 3:16; God gave his son.

Love sacrifices—John 15:13; Jesus sacrificed his life.

Love serves—Matthew 26:39; not *my* will but *thy* will be done.

Love considers—Ephesians 5:29; but nourishes and cherishes his flesh.

Love is both head and heart, felt and expressed, it is logic and emotion because love comes from the heart. Love is rooted in the character of God. He is, he does and he feels.

Love Never Ceases

I speak in the tongues of men and of angels, but have not love, I am a noisy gong or a clanging cymbal. And if I have prophetic powers, and understand all mysteries and all knowledge, and if I have all faith, so as to remove mountains, but have not love, I am nothing. If I give away all I have, and if I deliver up my body to be burned, but have not love, I gain nothing. Love is patient and kind; love does not envy or boast; it is not arrogant or rude. It does not insist on its own way; it is not irritable or resentful; it does not rejoice at wrongdoing, but rejoices with the truth. Love bears all things, believes all things, hopes all things, endures all things. Love never ends.

—1 Cor. 13:1–8

Love means more than anything we say. Even if we can say it in multiple languages, or speak the language of angels, if we do not have love, we are just talking noise. Love means more than anything we think. Having knowledge is great, especially if that knowledge is faith-based. But if we don't have love, all the knowledge in the world makes us nothing. Love means more than anything we do. We can give away everything we possess; we can help the poor and feed the hungry. Do it all without love, and we gain nothing.

If we love, then we can replace the word in the middle of the passage with our names. Do you love your spouse? If so, your name can be inserted when we read "love is patient and kind." Just continue from there with your name: "_____ does not envy or boast, is not arrogant or rude. _____ does not insist on [his or her] own way, is not irritable or resentful. _____ does not rejoice in wrongdoing but rejoices in the truth. _____ bears, believes, hopes, and endures." The next phrase is sobering: "Love never ends"!

Do you love your spouse? Have we ever loved our spouses? If we can fall out of love, it's possible we never had it. God never stops loving us because God is love. We could have placed God's name in the verses where the word occurs, and there would be no problem. God is patient and kind; he does not envy or boast. God is not irritable or resentful; he does not rejoice at wrongdoing but rejoices in truth.

We cannot blame our spouses for what we do and say. Husbands and wives often argue over what constitutes love. She does not always feel loved, and he is sure that he is behaving lovingly. Love is something you do, and what you do evokes feelings. Thus love is both done and felt.

Remember the love for a husband and wife is the same as loving God with all of our heart. The four parts of our heart won't allow us to argue over feelings or actions. In order to love with our whole heart we must include our intellect, emotion, conscience and will. Our knowledge of facts and our feelings based on those facts urge us to act in harmony with those things we believe. Then we take action and do; our will aligns all of our heart and others see our love.

Wrong, worldly thinking will never lead to spiritual living. We can't think like the world and live like God. Do you love your spouse like God teaches love?

18

LEARNING TO FORGIVE LIKE GOD

I f we could get married people to be honest with each other, the root of most of our problems is pain. Someone hurt someone else. The hurt was intensified precisely because of the unique relationship of marriage. There is no other relationship like it. And to fully understand it, you must be in or have been in it.

If only we could get past the hurt. If only that person would have hurt us just once. For many, they did get over the initial wound. But then more and more pain was caused. Please read these next words carefully.

The only scriptural way to live as God's child is to apply your life to him first and then apply it to people. Do you love God? Have you hurt God by sinning against him? Did he forgive you? Did you do it again? If we want to walk with God, commune with God, and live with God, we must learn to forgive like God.

Part of the trouble is the action or inaction of the ones who did the wrong. If they sinned against you, then they need to repent (Luke 17:3). This chapter is not about repentance; it is about forgiveness. When sin is committed, ideally the goal is reconciliation. Those who are estranged will be brought back together. There are three parts to this process.

In order to reconcile the one who sins must acknowledge the sin and repent. This usually involves an apology and a request to be forgiven. This is the part of the offender. For us to be reconciled to God, we must repent (Luke 13:3–5). The second part belongs to the one who was wronged. This person must forgive. In order to reconcile there must be forgiveness.

The end of both people doing their parts is reconciliation. The problem arises when one of the people won't do his or her part. For us, that generally means the one who sinned didn't repent fast enough, thoroughly enough, or we just didn't think the person meant it. While these things could be true, the problem is that the ones whose job it is to forgive misunderstands his responsibility.

This persons task is to forgive. But, instead of forgiving they assume another role. They become the quality control expert of repentance. This not the job of the person who was wronged your job is to forgive. You have taken God's job, he will judges heart. And when you are in his seat he judges you.

If the person did not meet their standards, they have a hard time forgiving. This is because we miss the powerful, amazing thing God did in forgiveness. When we fail to do the first thing God taught us, it starts us on a path of bitterness, pain, and burden-bearing that can last for years and decades maybe the rest of our life.

Let's focus on the first thing: those who are wronged. Go to the one who wronged you and seek reconciliation. Don't miss this. Don't go to tell the person off. Don't go because you finally got that person. Don't go because you are hurt. Go like God came to you when you sinned against him. Let's learn to forgive from God's example and then give forgiveness in our marriages.

When we learn to forgive, the forgiver will at last be free.

How to Forgive

Forgive Others as God Forgave You

> For if you forgive others their trespasses, your heavenly
> Father will also forgive you, but if you do not forgive

others their trespasses, neither will your Father forgive
your trespasses.

—Matthew 6:14–15

Let all bitterness and wrath and anger and clamor and
slander be put away from you, along with all malice.
Be kind to one another, tenderhearted, forgiving one
another, as God in Christ forgave you.

—Ephesians 4:31–32

Go to Those Who Sin against You, Offering Forgiveness

Moreover if thy brother shall trespass against thee, go
and tell him his fault between thee and him alone: if
he shall hear thee, thou hast gained thy brother.

—Matthew 18:15 KJV

When God is wronged—which is every time any sin is committed—he
approaches the offender, seeking reconciliation. Adam and Eve sinned
against God, and he went to them (Gen. 3:7–9). Cain sinned against
God, and God went to him (Gen. 4:1–8). The world sinned and grieved
God at his heart, and God, through Noah, went to the world (Gen.
6:1–8). Humanity sinned against God and Christ came to us.

If we want to learn to forgive like God, we must emulate this
trait. Don't wait until the offender comes to you; be like God and go
to them (Matt. 18:15–18). Don't go to someone else and talk about
them; instead, go to them alone. When you go, seek reconciliation,
not to get them told but to tell them you want the wrong fixed so the
relationship can continue. Make sure they know that your value of
the relationships is what brought you to them, not your anger of being wronged.

Paul describes God's actions in bringing Christ in terms of reconciliation:

> Therefore, if anyone is in Christ he is a new creation. The old has passed away; behold, the new has come. All this is from God, who through Christ reconciled us to himself and gave us the ministry of reconciliation; that is, in Christ God was reconciling the world to himself, not counting their trespasses against them, and entrusting to us the message of reconciliation. Therefore, we are ambassadors for Christ, God making his appeal through us. We implore you on behalf of Christ, be reconciled to God.
>
> —2 Corinthians 5:17–20

According to Strong's (e-sword.com) the word *reconciliation* means "exchange, fig. (adjustment) i.e., restoration to the (divine) favor: atonement, reconciliation."

Husbands and wives would do well to learn God's example. God was in Christ seeking to restore us to divine favor. He was sinned against, but he sought us and bought us by the blood of his son so we could be restored to him. How many couples need to hear Paul's impassioned plea, "We implore you on behalf of Christ, be reconciled to God"? We must make sure that we don't sin against God when others sin against us.

Forgive Swiftly

> Therefore if thou bring thy gift to the altar, and there rememberest that thy brother hath ought against thee; Leave there thy gift before the altar, and go thy way; first be reconciled to thy brother, and then come and offer thy gift. Agree with thine adversary quickly,

whiles thou art in the way with him; lest at any time the
adversary deliver thee to the judge, and the judge deliver thee to the officer, and thou be cast into prison.

—Matthew 5:23–25 KJV

Be ye angry, and sin not: let not the sun go down upon
your wrath: Neither give place to the devil.

—Ephesians 4:26–27

When we sin against God and repent, we don't have to wait for forgiveness; God forgives. The Lord gives us insight into how quickly we
should seek to make things right. If we are at worship and remember
that a brother is offended, we are to stop worshipping God. The Lord
is effectively saying, "I'll wait; go fix the problem and come back and
worship me."

Paul gives a three-step problem that can end badly if we don't fix
things quickly. First, be angry, but second, don't allow your anger to
cause you to sin. If you have a situation, don't let the sun go down
before you resolve the issue because, third, delay gives opportunity
to the devil. The more time and distance that get between problems
and solutions. Only serves to make the offense stronger and the offender seem more wicked. Time and distance work against the idea
of forgiveness. So God says forgive quickly, don't let the sun go down.
Forgive while you have molehills not mountains.

Forgive without Exception

For when we were yet without strength, in due time
Christ died for the ungodly. For scarcely for a righteous
man will one die: yet peradventure for a good man
some would even dare to die. But God commended

his love toward us, in that, while we were yet sinners,
Christ died for us.

—Romans 5:6–8

We cannot have big sins that we cannot forgive because God does not.
He will forgive any sin; the list of sins in scripture bears this out (Rom.
1:18–32; 1 Cor. 6:9–11). It is not easy, but if we are willing to forgive
every sin, it will be easier for us to forgive the last sin and the next sin.

God sent Christ when we were weak, ungodly sinners. We couldn't
get lower; we couldn't get worse. So why would we think our offender
should be perfect before we can forgive? Sinners are the ones who
need forgiveness, not the righteous. If they didn't wrong you, you
wouldn't need to forgive them. Of course, the same could be said
about us toward God. But we did wrong him, and he forgave us. The
only question is, will we do the same?

Don't Keep a List

> The Lord is merciful and gracious, slow to anger and
> abounding in steadfast love. He will not always chide,
> nor will he keep his anger forever. He does not deal
> with us according to our sins, nor repay us according
> to our iniquities. For as high as the heavens are above
> the earth, so great is his steadfast love toward those
> who fear him; as far as the east is from the west, so far
> does he remove our transgressions from us.

—Psalm 103:8–12

God does not keep a running tally of sins against him. When he forgives, he removes them as far as the east is from the west. He is merciful; he tempers his judgment, giving us less than we deserve. He is

gracious, extending his favor to us even though we sinned against him. He is slow to anger and does not keep his anger forever.

In order to help our marriages and help ourselves, we must learn to forgive others the way God forgives us. Carrying around pain, hurt, and anger leads to resentment, irritability, and frustration. Living like this makes us miserable. Our marriages are to be places of safety, security, and serenity. How sad that many marriages are the source of the involved parties' greatest pain and sorrow. This is not what God intended when he saw Adam alone in the garden. Learning to forgive can be the blessing that our marriages need.

God forgives you; will you forgive your spouse? Mentally tear up the list of sins you have been keeping against you and free yourself.

Forgive from the Heart

> Then Peter came up and said to him, "Lord how often
> will my brother sin against me, and I forgive him? As
> many as seven times?" Jesus said to him, "I do not say
> to you seven times, but seventy times seven."

> —Matthew 18:21–22

The Lord gave a parable following this question from Peter. The parable was about a king who called his servant to settle an account with him. The servant was in debt to the king for a sum that he could not pay. Most estimate he couldn't have repaid his debt within several lifetimes. Because of his inability to pay, the king sentenced him to sell everything he owned. Even his wife and children were punished until payment could be made.

Unable to pay and hearing the sentence, the servant fell down and begged the king for mercy. The king was moved with compassion and forgave the debt. The same servant left the king and found a fellow servant who owed him a little money. The same interchange happened. The fellow servant fell down at his feet and pled for mercy.

Instead of being moved with compassion, the forgiven servant put his fellow servant in jail. Other servants witnessed this exchange and told the king all that had happened. Upon hearing this, the king called the servant he had forgiven back into his presence. It is what happens next that must teach us all how God expects us to forgive:

> Then his master summoned him and said to him, You wicked servant! I forgave you all that debt because you pleaded with me. And should not you have had mercy on your fellow servant, as I had mercy on you. And in anger his master delivered him to the jailers, until he should pay all his debt. So also my heavenly Father will do to every one of you, if you do not forgive your brother from your heart.
>
> —Matthew 18:32–35

This parable is the result of Peter's question; the Lord's first answer was that forgiveness has no limit: "Not seven times but seventy times seven" or, in other words, without limit, Peter. In the parable, it is easy to understand that we are the first servant. We have all sinned against God, and if called upon to account for ourselves, every one of us has a debt against God we cannot pay.

God in Christ forgave our sins. He (not we) erased our debt. Christ is the Lamb of God who takes away the sin of the world (John 1:29). We needed him to forgive us because there was nothing we could do on our own, and he did. Now, God, through this parable, gives us insight and clarity into his view of us when others sin against us and we refuse to forgive.

It is sobering and should create in us reverent fear. His words should rattle around in our minds until we find no comfort from the sound: "I forgave you all that debt because you pleaded with me. And should not you have had mercy on your fellow servant, as I had mercy on you? So also my heavenly Father will do to every one of you, if you do not forgive your brother from your heart."

If we refuse to forgive others, God will refuse to forgive us. He expressly told us this in his Word. May we all believe him. Is the pain you're holding onto worth heaven to you? God forgave us; we must forgive others. Marriage is heaven's gift to humanity; may you have all the joy that God intended in yours.

For my wife and me, September 2015 marked twenty-seven years of marriage. We have given each other great joy, and we have caused each other immense pain. We have been married. If we will be blessed to make another twenty-seven and beyond, we must forgive. Everyone hurts and gets hurt. Those who love the Lord and emulate his actions overcome the pain.

They don't ignore it. Neither do they pretend wrongdoing didn't happen. Instead, they look toward their God and see his perfectness. They know they've hurt him and that he forgave them. They see themselves, and they reject the desire to be self-righteous. They don't blame, point fingers, or call names.

If they did the wrong, they repent and ask for forgiveness. If they were wronged, they go and inform their spouses, seeking reconciliation. They draw a line in the sand and move forward, striving to live like the God who gave them marriage and forgave their sins.

Marriage is possibly the greatest blessing God gave humanity. We can never be closer to another human being on earth. God didn't leave us alone. He gave us a partner for life to help us return home to him and live in heaven. Thank God for marriage.

19

TEN TIPS FOR FOR HUSBANDS AND WIVES

These tips are not in order of importance even though they are numbered. The tips have been gleaned from conversations with men and women. Nothing is intended to be offensive it is what people have said to me or sentiments I have heard expressed. We don't always tell each other our true feelings. However women tell women and men tell men, what they really feel while both often hold back from telling their spouses.

Maybe it is our desire to be politically correct or we fear we might hurt our spouses feelings. Unfortunately since we do think and feel these things we end up living with them in our marriages. Often we "suffer" in silence without ever saying anything to the person we love. Putting our spouse in a near impossible situation. They can't fix the problem if they don't even know it is a problem. Additionally, there is a bonus tip for husbands and wives at the end concerning faithfulness.

With these things in mind these tips are offered. I hope they help or maybe start a conversation.

Practical Tips for Wives

1. **If you are unwilling to try and lose weight, stop talking about it.**
    When you mention your disappointment with your weight to your husband, he believes you will start taking action to

fix your perceived problem. If you don't do something to lose weight after acknowledging a problem and your desire, you lose credibility with your husband.

Nearly every part of our lives that we desire to improve requires action. If your clothes don't fit as they once did, you have two options. Buy a bigger size or take action to change your size. If you choose the third option of constantly talking about it, over time your husband will grow weary and wonder why you bother saying it all.

Losing weight is exceedingly difficult success involves healthy eating, lots of water and exercise. It also involves consuming less sugar and more fruits and vegetables. Anyone who has tried knows how hard it is. The point is not to minimize the difficulty of losing weight it is to discourage talking without changing. Talk is cheap. Maybe worse, it is dishonest and disingenuous.

2. **Lose the girdle, Spanx, and other similar items.**

Your husband has seen you without your clothes. He knows. His desire is not that you find a way to make yourself look smaller. If he is interested in you being smaller, he actually wants you smaller, not the appearance of it. This is closely connected to number one. Instead of talking, some women opt for covering or hiding.

Your husband is not simply interested in your physical appearance. He is—but not totally. He is interested in the spirit of the person who acknowledges a problem. But instead of you doing what it takes to solve it, she talks about it, covers it, or hides it. Once the covering is on he is often asked, "How do I look?" It takes a careful man to solve this puzzle correctly.

At the same time, you demand that he actually make changes in his life, and you should. You don't just want him to talk about issues in his life. Neither do you want him to try to mask them. When he acknowledges his issues, you expect him to fix them and this is the proper expectation. Like him, you would rather he actually work on his issues and make the necessary changes. Your husband may not tell you but he thinks you don't keep your word.

3. **Get dressed for your husband, not others.**

Women tend to dress up for work to look good for their fellow employees. Often they get dressed for other women. If other women think you look good, what is that to you? Your husband wants to see you look good, and often your good looks are wasted on everyone else, but him.

Doing things is not the same as doing things for your husband. It is popular to suggest that you are not getting dressed or losing weight for your husband. But, if you are not looking good for him, then who is it for? If you say for yourself, then why haven't you done it? Surely, you love yourself enough to take care of your health. If your husband is not worth the effort, do you think he knows that, and how should he feel about it?

4. **Ask the question you want answered.**

Questions are mostly used for information gathering. If you want to know something, ask. But every husband knows when he is being led by the questions. And when the questions turn to interrogations, husbands will get short with their answers or shut down completely. It may not always be easy, but be careful here; your husband will feel sabotaged.

5. **Embrace your role.**

God, not man, established the roles of husbands and wives. Your husband does not want to fight about who is the leader. Your role is to help. If you view your role as a burden, your husband will know it. If you complain about his decision making and leadership, he will feel undermined. If you try to lead from behind he will feel like a puppet with you holding the strings. Nothing will make him happier than to know you don't simply support him but that you want to support him.

6. **Consider your words.**

   Some wives are rude, and sometimes they insult their husbands. Because men are thought to be tough and strong, often his feelings are not considered. Sadly he doesn't speak feelings; which is bad for him and unfair to you. Still, rarely are wives called on their sarcastic, harsh speech. Questioning his intelligence, talking down to him, or speaking slowly is not helpful. He feels the hurt; if he doesn't say anything, he is storing the memory, and it will affect his view of you. It is not right but it happens.

7. **Be open to sexual adventure.**

   Sex is not slavery, nor is anyone ever to be abused. But if he wants to try new things, be open to them. It is important to continue to grow in all aspects of your relationship. Done correctly, new things can add variety and new experiences that you both enjoy. Closing the door with an emphatic no to anything new or different will hurt, not help. The problem won't be the item in question. The problem will be that one of you made a decision for both of you. Whenever this happens, the other person feels slighted.

   Sex should not be viewed as love, it is a special event within a marriage where love is already present. Make advances toward your husband sometimes don't just wait until he asks for sex. If you want to know when he is ready, the answer is always but over time he will grow weary of having to ask. If he always has to ask it will appear that you are not interested but simply doing him a favor or performing a wifely duty. God placed sex within marriage it should be enjoyed by both people.

8. **Strive to be consistent.**

   Your husband is going to do wrong, and so will you. When you do wrong, don't make yours less than his. Try to be consistent in your treatment of your actions and his. Men and women are prone to count their spouses' actions as worse than their own. When we hold our spouses to a higher standard, they begin to watch us and wait for us to do wrong so they can feel justified in bringing it to our attention.

9. **Be a lady.**

You are not a man. You can be strong, but you must not lose your femininity. God made a woman and brought her to the man. Women are special because they are women. While doing your hair and makeup may be important to you and others, it is your sweet, meek, and gentle spirit that is important and beautiful to your husband. It won't matter how good you look physically. If you are loud, stubborn, and difficult, you will be ugly to your husband. Solomon thought it was better to live in a rooftop than with an argumentative and contentious woman.

10. **Remember 1 Corinthians 7:34.**

"But she that is married careth for the things of the world, how she may please her husband." It is God's design and desire that married people seek to please each other. It is easy to live for yourself, others, and your children. You are married to only one person, your husband. Let your actions be motivated by love. Love for God first, love for self-second, and love for your husband next. No one else should come before your husband. Pleasing him should be the goal; he is your husband.

Practical Tips for Husbands

1. **Have a plan and share it with your wife.**

   Your wife needs certainty. She needs to know where you are leading her. Without a plan, you cannot arrive at a destination. A plan known by you but unknown to her is unsettling to her. God never told anyone to follow a leader who didn't have a plan to lead. Why would you ask of your wife to do what God has never asked of anyone? No one wants to follow someone who does not know where he is going. You don't either.

2. **Consider your wife's feelings.**

   Saying men are logical does not mean that men have no feelings. Men feel, and they know that their wives have feelings. So consider deeply how your actions make your wife feel. You can argue about your actions and what you meant, or you can consider how your actions made her feel.

   Live so she knows you had her feelings in mind before you acted. Even if the action is right, how she feels is still very important. What you did will probably be secondary to how your actions made her feel. Please don't argue this, consider your wife's feelings before you act.

3. **Protect your wife.**

   Your wife does not want you in a fistfight. But she does want to know that you would fight for her. She needs to feel secure emotionally, physically, and spiritually. Put everyone else on notice that your wife is your first priority. No one should feel comfortable putting your wife down unchecked. Scripture says we should be willing to die for our wives. God meant it, and everyone else should know you mean it as well. Most of all, your wife should know it. If you don't protect her see # 2 how does that make her feel?

4. **Consider your words.**

   "Sticks and stones may break my bones, but words will never hurt me." There are big lies, and then there is this one.

Your words are among the most powerful tools in your relationship toolbox. Your wife believes in you and trusts you. She has struggles in her own life that she is working on. But she has entrusted her heart to you. This is very precious cargo, please handle with care – I mean great care.

If you use your words to hurt your wife, you can cause irreparable damage to the very person you vowed your never-ending love to. God compared words to fire, swords, and poison and words are said to be able to cause death and give life. How would you use any of these items toward your wife? Be exceedingly mindful of your words. Before you speak see # 2 consider her feelings.

If necessary apologize to your wife. Don't apologize when you are not wrong but don't miss an opportunity to give a heartfelt apology when necessary. When apologizing take time don't do it when you or your wife are busy. Take your time don't rush through an apology. Make eye contact, if the eyes are the windows of the soul then let her look deeply into yours as you peer deeply into hers. Share your heart felt feelings about causing your bride pain.

Never suggest it was her fault, she is too sensitive or that if she felt offended that you are sorry she felt that way. Your words in an apology are as powerful as the words that made an apology necessary. Never miss a good opportunity to apologize well. It means so much and it can mend deep wounds.

5. **Avoid hypocrisy.**

Leaders are held to a higher standard. Deal with it and please get over it. Your words are more significant precisely because you are the leader. If God is against anything, it is hypocritical leaders. Hypocrisy occurs when we say one thing and do another. It also occurs when we ask something of others that we refuse to do ourselves. Christ condemns both in Matthew 23:1-6.

Jesus never asked us to do anything he didn't do. So make sure you don't do this to your wife. If you want kind speech lead your family in speaking kindly. The same is true for fairness, love and edification. How do you feel when your boss or fellow employees say one thing and do another? Leaders lead, they don't just bark out instructions. God's man does not live by the motto, "do as I say not as I do." Instead he would say, "follow me as I follow Christ."

6. **Be a man.**

The world has it wrong; we are not unisex. We are different, and she needs the differences you possess. Do the things a man should do for his wife. Pull out her chair and open her door. Tell her you love her and show her more. Talk is cheap when men do it also. Make sure she knows her man loves her and will take care of her.

Take out the trash, help around the house, and set the tone for her and the children. Make sure the world knows your wife is not alone; she has a God-fearing man who loves her, will stand up for her and next to her. A wife is better when her husband behaves like God's man instead of the world's new woman or some glorified child.

7. **Take care of your health.**

Round is a shape, but it is not very attractive; neither is it healthy. Your wife wants you around for a long time. So go to the doctor, get a physical, take vitamins, and take care of yourself. Men's sex drives start to dip as they get older, just about the time women's start to rise. Wash yourself before sex. More importantly, keep yourself healthy enough for her to enjoy sex with you. You owe her someone to be attracted to as well. Consider your shape if you are ever tempted to talk about hers. Many round men want a small well figured woman is that hypocritical?

8. **Help rear the children and help around the house.**

The house belongs to both of you. The children are your children as well. Faithful fathers lead their children and help their wives. Both set a wonderful example for your children. Your son learns how a man leads his family. Your daughter learns how a man loves his wife. If your wife is tired from working either outside or inside the house or both, sex will be a chore instead of a joy. Help yourself and your children by helping your wife. Absentee fathers don't always leave the home.

9. **Embrace your role.**

You are a husband. It is among the greatest things one can do with his life. You emulate Christ. You have won a woman's heart—the greatest prize ever won. Go to work; support your family. You are their leader. Steer the ship, pilot the plane, and help the family arrive safely on heaven's shore. I've heard it said that they are yours for a while so they can be God's forever. Get help if you need it. Asking for help is not a sign of weakness it is a sign of strength and wisdom. If the world gets you they are more likely to get your family.

10. **Remember 1 Corinthians 7:33.**

"But he that is married careth for the things that are of the world, how he may please his wife." Give her your love. Laugh with her, enjoy her, and share your life with her. She wants your dreams to come true. Be her husband, champion her, and lift her up. Grow up and grow old with this wondrously beautiful woman. God believes you will aim to please her. Make sure you do. She is your wife and God's daughter. Treat God's daughter the way you would want a man to treat your daughter.

A Bonus Tip for Husbands and Wives

Don't Cheat!

The Bible warns us not to cheat, but, like many warnings God gives, this one often goes unheeded. Sin is sin, we are told. In a sense, that is true. If one sins against God, any sin is sufficient to harm the relationship with him because God cannot fellowship any amount of sin (1 John 1:5–10). In this sense, sin is sin, and one is not worse than another.

But sin is not sin in this regard—the harm it causes, the trust it breaks, and the difficulty it brings. Every sin does not have the same effect in the lives of the sinner or the one sinned against. There is no relationship like marriage. No relationship is as close as marriage. No relationship costs us more and no relationship asks as much of us than marriage. This is why nothing is so harmful to a marriage as infidelity.

The warnings in scripture are legion. Read in one sitting Proverbs chapters 5–7. Read also Ezekiel 16 and the first four chapters of Hosea. This is just a sampling of the material in scripture concerning unfaithfulness in a marital relationship. The list of sins God's children are told to avoid always includes sins of a sexual nature. Passages like 1 Corinthians 6:9–11 and Galatians 5:19–21 are two powerful examples. To the saints in Ephesus, Paul wrote that fornication was never once to be named among them (Eph. 5:3).

You can only be Superman or Wonder Woman once. If you cheat, you will likely never again be the hero your spouse once thought you were. If you come to yourself, you will try to repair the damage. God will forgive, and your spouse will do the best they can to forgive as well. But maybe they won't even know that something in them died when you cheated.

They will want the marriage to be the same as it was before the cheating, and so will you. The problem is your marriage is not the same. Let us all remember this; *we are never the same after sin as we were before sin.* Sin costs; sin changes us; and it changes the circumstances and conditions of life. Adam and Eve were not the same after they sinned. David was not the same after he sinned with Bathsheba.

The problem with wanting the marriage to be the same as it was is you did more than cheat. Cheaters have a vested interest in hiding what they are doing. This interest causes them to do more than cheat. The cheater often lies to his spouse. The lies along with the cheating erode the foundation of the relationship.

The lying, sneaking around, and keeping secrets cause the spouse to see the cheater differently before the cheating is ever discovered. When the cheating is at last acknowledged or no longer deniable, the cheater thinks the worst is over. In truth, the real battle has just begun.

As the cheater attempts to repair the relationship, he/she focuses on the cheating itself. He moves from apologetic and sorrowful to defiant and angry. The cheater almost demands that things get back to the way they were. He might even say, "I said I was sorry." Sadly, he knows nothing of how dramatically, possibly even unalterably, he has changed his marriage.

He has no idea that every time his spouse sees him, all of the pain is present—not just the cheating but also the lying, the deception, the denials, and how often his spouse was made out to be the bad person. He will never know that his spouse knew he was cheating much earlier than he confessed.

He won't know how often she went through the day trying to be happy with a broken heart. Because he was the cheater, and not the one being cheated on, he will never know the other side. When she looks at him, she replays days, weeks, and months in her head in an instant. She thinks about the times she had sex with him while knowing he was having sex with someone else.

When he tries to get things back to the way they were, he will have no idea of the task before him. Though he won't believe it, his spouse won't have any idea either. She may even want it to be and wish it could be. But try as she might, she can't make her eyes see something other than what they see.

All is not lost, the good news is they can have a healthy, happy relationship again, but it will be different. You can be Clark Kent, but more than likely Superman or Wonder Woman has died, cheating is kryptonite to marriage.

What the cheater doesn't know is that he or she will spend his or her life trying to once again be the superhero. Very sadly, that person will one day discover that he or she can never fly again. Your spouse is not to be blamed. He or she will want you to fly and wish that you could fly again. But when superheroes lose their powers, they become just regular people. This is okay; it's just different. Maybe we should never have been superheroes in the first place.

Cheating on your spouse is not the unpardonable sin, but it will certainly change your marriage.

20

THE COUPLE THAT _____
TOGETHER THRIVES TOGETHER

A great word for marriage is together. Two have become one and they have been joined to each other. The concept of together should remain a constant for husbands and wives in marriage. Consider the Lord's statement. "A house divided against itself cannot stand. . . " (Matt. 12:25). Sit down together take a piece of paper and you and your spouse write down things that are important to you. Things like money, rearing children, time, housework, vacation, spirituality and any other thing you think important. Write them all down and ask yourselves on which of these are we together?

You didn't get married to remain single. If you don't agree, you can't walk together. I will tell you a little secret. It really doesn't matter what we do together, as long as we are **together.**

The couple that prays together thrives together - What better way to help and enrich each other than by praying to God for and with each other. If you pray for anyone pray for yourself, your spouse and your family first then pray for others. What will God think if you pray to him for everyone else more than you pray for your spouse?

The couple that plays together thrives together - Don't fool yourself, making friends apart from your spouse while having fun can lead to ruin. If there were one person to have fun with in your life who better than your spouse? Your heart goes into having fun don't give any of your heart to another, have fun together.

The couple that shares together thrives together - Do you want fuel to propel you forward in your life. Then share your hopes, desires and fears with your spouse. You will want to help each other reach them. Sadly, many married people dream and are afraid alone. Let each other into your hearts.

The couple that dreams together thrives together - Write your story together. Your past is gone, your future is ahead of you so write your dreams in the present. You both will be committed to making them come true with and for each other. We, is one of the great words in marriage. We planned, we prepared and we accomplished our dreams together.

The couple that worships together thrives together - "Can two walk together accept they agree?" This is God's question to his people and it is a great question for husbands and wives. God and his word shapes our thoughts, determines our beliefs and establishes our morals. We need to be together spiritually, united in Christ through obedience to the gospel. We can give each other tremendous help as well as grace, mercy and forgiveness as we both strive to emulate our heavenly Father. Christ is the standard for husbands as the church is for wives.

The couple that saves/spends together thrives together - Money is not the root of all evil but the love of money is. Don't allow money to ruin your marriage. A great way to avoid financial troubles is to be together concerning your money. First, see it as "our money." I've rarely heard of separate bank accounts working well for married people. We can't be united in everything but money. Second, be wise and allow the person who is best with the money to be the primary manager of your money. Third, be open and honest about money. Don't hide it, waste it or use it against each other. Money is paper (cloth) it has neither mind nor soul. It is a tool so use it wisely together. Don't allow an inanimate, lifeless piece of paper to ruin your marriage.

The couple that disciplines together thrives together - Children need parents not just one. So develop a game plan for how you will rear your children. Don't always make one parent the bad guy while the other always seeks to be the good guy. If the parents are together the children will hear one voice and a consistent message. But, if the parents are not together their children will use their division and conquer them. Don't lose your marriage for your children. If we are together, nothing can break us apart. If we are divided our house cannot stand.

CONCLUSION

Remember our alien visitor, we met at the beginning of our journey? After delving deeply into God's word he would now know what marriage is. And because he knows what marriage is, he would also know who God is. He would also know that our very existence as humans is the result of marriage. According to Genesis 1, man was married on the first day of his existence. Adam and Eve were made and married on the sixth day. This means humanity has never lived a day without marriage.

Marriage is the greatest relationship we have on earth; it has perpetuated our existence. Because our alien visitor now knows what marriage is, he would also know our Lord Jesus Christ. He would understand that the great mystery of God revealed in Scripture is about Christ and his church. The illustration to mirror Christ's matchless love for the church is marriage. Husbands love your wives even as Christ loved the church, and wives see that you reverence your husband, is God's divine wisdom.

Our alien friend would leave knowing that marriage is where children are to be born and reared. He would see in marriage God's design for the continuance of the human race. God intended for children to learn, from watching their parents' marriage, how to one day live in their own marriages then teach their children about him and so on and so on.

Because he knows God's design, he would know that God made one man and one woman for each other for life. What a blessing to walk through life together praising and pleasing God. Husbands and wives should see their marriage through the eyes of God. May his love for his people be the love husbands have for their wives. And may his people's devotion and reverence for God be the same as wives toward their husbands. Let's make our marriages a relationship that glorifies God and illuminates the path for others to find him.

God's greatest blessing to humanity is Christ on the cross. Second to the spiritual blessings of Christ is the relationship of marriage. Marriage typifies Christ's relationship with his church and expresses God's love for his people. In marriage a man represents Christ, and a woman represent Christ's bride the church.

To take marriage is to take God - *Do you take God?*

It is not good that the man should be alone; I will make him a help suitable for him.

—God

OTHER WORKS BY THE AUTHOR

Eric has written two other books, "*So you want to be happy.*" In it he tells us that happiness is spiritual not physical. The wise Solomon undertook a search for meaning and fulfillment under the sun. His conclusion was "vanity of vanities all is vanity." When one searches under the sun this is the only conclusion that can be reached. Because, happiness is not under the sun, it is beyond the sun. Only God through Christ can make us happy, but we must have a spiritual approach to God to reap his spiritual blessings.

His second book, "*So you want to be happy*" – *Teens.*" In it he takes his military background and weaves it through Bible lessons for God's spiritual solders. Solders must obey their commanding officer, they must honor their calling and persevere to win the victory. Eric compares the duties, responsibilities and training of the Marines with God's spiritual service for his solders. The great thing about God's army is because of Christ we are assured the victory. The book is for teens and young adults, great for youth groups and Bible classes.

Made in the USA
Middletown, DE
29 September 2021